"The Loecken family doesn't just believe our national creed...'that all men are created equal'...they live it. Their actions affirm the dignity of those in need, and their story will inspire you to do the same."

—**Dr. John Perkins,** pastor, social entrepreneur, author of *Let Justice Roll Down*

"This book is one more sign of a movement of revolutionary love that is spreading across the earth. Christians like the Loecken family are beginning to take Jesus seriously again and to abandon the empty promises of materialism for the winsome freedom of the lilies and the sparrows. They are not judgmental, idealistic, or naive—they have simply found a Pearl that is worth leaving all the counterfeit splendor of this world to pursue. May their courage comfort those of us who are afflicted and afflict those of us who are comfortable."

—**Shane Claiborne**, author, activist, and recovering sinner

"Jay and Beth Loecken's lives were changed after a missions trip to Africa showed them the importance of human relationships and the uselessness of our earthly possessions. They sold everything they owned and embarked on a tour performing random acts of kindness to all that they met. Their amazing story will inspire you to appreciate the simple joy of serving others."

—**Pastor Matthew Barnett**, co-founder of the Dream Center

"The Loecken family lives on purpose. This book which tells their story will inspire you because they embody biblical passion and pursue relationships intentionally, courageously, and authentically. I have spent hours with Jay and Beth and I can assure you— they are the real deal. The ideas in this book will move you to transform your passions into action, just as they did."

—**Dr. Tim Elmore**, President of GrowingLeaders.com, author of *Generation iY*

"We all say that we're serious about the gospel, but Jay and Beth Loecken actually live it out. They have sacrificed all the things we think are so important, like a house, a new car, PTA membership, and status, to live out the gospel and make it real in the lives of thousands of people. This book may just change the way you think about being a Christian."

—**Phil Cooke,** filmmaker, media consultant, and author of *Jolt!*

"Most of us take Jesus' words with a grain of salt. After all, He asked for some pretty extreme commitment. Well, Jay and Beth Loecken and family are not those people. They have sold out and bought in. They threw caution and comfort to the wind and bet the farm, literally, that following Jesus was the adventure they wanted to live. Goodbye house, hello RV. You're going to want to read their story. Better yet, you're going to want to meet this family."

—**Terry Esau**, author of *Be the Surprise: Experiments in Spontaneous Faith*

"It is encouraging to see a family actually living out their faith rather than just talking about it. My prayer is that everyone who reads this book will realize that His plans are so much better than our plans. God will rarely (if ever) give you the whole plan for your life up front, but He will tell you what the next step is if you ask Him sincerely, listen for His answer (and His timing), and then do what He tells you to do. Obedience equals freedom. Thank you, Jay, Beth, Ben, Bekah, Abigail, and Noah, for being salt and light across America."

— **Janine Maxwell,** co-founder of Heart for Africa and
author of and *Is It Okay with You?*

"Our church has been forever changed as a result of having the Passion to Action bus stop over in our parking lot for a weekend. The Loecken family challenged our congregation and we were inspired by their story and mission of mercy, sacrifice, and service. We have been mobilized to 'get out of our building' and embrace the unique opportunity God has given us to make an eternal difference in our neighborhood."

— **Dan Johnson,** senior pastor, Plymouth Covenant Church, Plymouth, Minnesota

"Preaching 'love your neighbor' is easy. Actually loving your neighbor like Jesus told us to do is authentic discipleship. Jay, Beth, and the kids have reminded me what real love and obedience to Jesus is."

— **Jeff Evans,** pastor, The Vine Church, Rancho Cucamonga, California

"Jay and Beth Loecken are a delight and their story is an inspiration. Jump in with joyful expectancy!"

— **David W. Henderson,** senior pastor,
Covenant Church, West Lafayette, Indiana

"We recently had the Loecken family in our church for a Passion to Action weekend. It was one of the most encouraging and yet challenging weekends we have experienced. Jay, Beth, and the children were a blessing. They showed us what it means to put your faith in action and as a result we had seventy people go out and serve others in our city. The passion, simplicity, and authenticity of the Loecken family was refreshing and encouraging to me as a pastor. I encourage you to prayerfully consider having the Loeckens share their lives with your church or ministry. Warning: you and your people may never be the same."

— **Greg Salyer**, pastor, Discovery Pointe Church, Phoenix, Arizona

JAY & BETH LOECKEN
WITH LAURA MORTON

Guideposts
New York, New York

Passion 2 Action

ISBN-10: 0-8249-4857-2
ISBN-13: 978-0-8249-4857-3

Published by Guideposts
16 East 34th Street
New York, New York 10016
Guideposts.org

Distributed by Ideals Publications, a Guideposts company
2636 Elm Hill Pike, Suite 120
Nashville, TN 37214

Guideposts and *Ideals* are registered trademarks of Guideposts.

ACKNOWLEDGMENTS

Every attempt has been made to credit the sources of copyrighted material used in this book. If any such acknowledgment has been inadvertently omitted or miscredited, receipt of such information would be appreciated.

All Scripture quotations are taken from *The Holy Bible, New International Version.* Copyright © 1973, 1978, 1984 International Bible Society. Used by permission of Zondervan Bible Publishers.

Library of Congress Cataloging-in-Publication Data has been applied for.

Cover design by Morsekode
Cover photograph by Mike Huffstatler
Interior design by Müllerhaus
Typeset by Müllerhaus

Printed and bound in the United States of America
10 9 8 7 6 5 4 3 2 1

"The Loecken family mission is, first, to love God with all of our heart, soul, mind, and strength and then to love each other by doing acts of random kindness in our own family first and then for others."

Created October 25, 2008
Portland, Oregon

To our four amazing children: Ben, Bekah, Abigail, and Noah, for your undying commitment to a life of service and for your support, encouragement, and laughter along the way. Our lives are richer because of each of you.

To the unsung heroes who serve tirelessly day in and day out with little or no recognition. Your reward will be great in eternity.

CONTENTS

PREFACE

This is a book that describes our journey of passion, faith, and taking action to serve others. It is a story of self-discovery from how one big decision ultimately led us to finding hope, fulfillment, and our true purpose and meaning in life. The many adventures we've shared not only brought us closer to God, they also connected us as a family in ways we could not have imagined before we set out and hit the road.

As you read, you'll also see that we've summed up 10 essential challenges that each of us must face as we seek to discover ways to put our passion to action. We encourage you to take the P2A Challenges to heart and explore their possibilities for your own life.

Throughout the text you will see that we've divided our story into three different voices—Beth, Jay, and our collective words. We've indicated who is writing at the top of each section so you will be able to follow. Where there is no identification, it is our collective voice.

We do not hold the pen to write our faith story. God is the author of that. It is only when we give up control and allow Him full access to our lives that He can do His best work.

As we have given Him the little we have—our five loaves and two fish—He has the power to multiply it and do so much more than we ever imagined.

This is our story and how we came to understand the power of God and the great strength in faith.

1 · THERE HAD TO BE MORE

DECEMBER 2006
ATLANTA, GEORGIA

BETH» Something unsettling had been stirring in our hearts for a very long time. We both knew we wanted—no, make that needed—something more out of life than what we had already achieved. By all definitions, we were living the good life: privileged and full of prosperity. Jay's business as a mortgage broker had afforded us a very comfortable lifestyle. We owned a forty-five-hundred-square-foot house in Alpharetta, Georgia, that was our dream home—right down to the perfect and beautifully landscaped backyard we had just finished putting the final touches on.

Although we weren't wealthy, we were quite comfortable. We were actively involved in our church, had a great family life, and were living a pretty good existence. Our four children didn't have to wear secondhand clothes. We were able to take the entire family to the movies and out to dinner whenever we wanted to without thinking about the cost. We pretty much had the ability to have whatever we wanted at the drop of a hat.

Along with our home, we owned two cars, a motorcycle, and were close to purchasing a new boat and convertible BMW. For years we gave ourselves almost every luxury a family like ours could hope for.

Our lifestyle had become what you might think of as ideal—the American dream personified. Yet with all of the success we had achieved, and although we were generally happy, we were not feeling fulfilled. There was a void in us—an emptiness that living only for oneself brings. We weren't comfortable living caught up in what other people thought of us.

While Jay was making loads of money, we trusted in our finances instead of God. If or when we had a need, it was taken care of without a thought.

We were living the dream—right?

The only problem was that we no longer needed to depend on God. It was easy to stop trusting in Him for provision and relying on Him for our needs. Our relationship with Jesus became less desperate and, at times, stagnant.

Four years of living the dream and still, we couldn't shake an ever-present feeling that kept tugging at Jay and me.

Simply said, we knew there had to be more; but we had absolutely no idea what it was we were looking for.

There was a void, a longing, an empty place deep inside of us that seemed to quietly whisper that our lives were missing "something." We thought the something was more stuff. We had struggled financially for years prior to coming to Atlanta, and the fact that we could buy new furniture and make all the updates to our home without a thought felt good. We thought the something that was missing from our previous financially strapped life was things: a comfortable lifestyle, kids in sports, nice clothes, a nice neighborhood, and a settled life. The only problem was that once those things were all purchased or attained, they seemed to breed more discontent. One purchase or update led to another and it went on and on. The something was never filled; in fact, material things seemed to make the ache grow deeper because they caused us to realize that we would never be filled that way.

When our life would finally quiet down (typically on a Sunday), and after hearing a great message at church, we would follow the thousands of others who filed out of church, jump in our nice car, and head home. But we began to notice a deep loneliness and hollowness. We felt sadly alone, empty, and purposeless. We never felt this way when our life was hurried and chaotic. In fact, when we noticed the emptiness creeping in, we would busy ourselves around the house, cleaning, organizing, "doing" so that we didn't have to answer the ever-noticeable voice we both heard calling to us. In many ways, we didn't want to face the questions that were rising up inside of us.

Did our lives matter?

What were our goals?

Is this really the abundant life?

What are we craving?

The ache was not there in the beginning; but as our dream life ended up not being the big deal that we thought it would be, it began to grow and grow in our hearts. I think we glamorized what having money would be like. I believe we thought that all of our financial worries would be over, all of our longings would be fulfilled, our hearts would be content, and our relationships would be rich. That couldn't have been further from the truth. The more we owned, the more stress and responsibility we had. The more things we filled our life up with, the less time we had for deep relationships.

Once we had money, we stopped praying about whether to purchase items.

It was simple, did we want it? Check.

Did we have the perfect location in our house for it? Check.

Could we afford it? Check.

Our evaluation process did not involve God in any way. Our needs were met simply by Jay working harder and longer hours. The harder he worked, the bigger his paycheck was. We made sacrifices and began to place money and material things in front of family time and our marriage. I didn't get upset or nag him when he would come home at eight o'clock when the kids were slipping into bed—because, selfishly, I wanted to live the life we were living. I wanted to be able to finish our basement and drive a nice car. It was a vicious cycle, and it slowly began to chip away at the foundation of our marriage and family. When times are good, you think they will always be good and you often don't or can't see what's around the corner.

But something clicked when we started to think about the dreams for authentic living that we had given up. We somehow saw that what was happening was the complete opposite. We realized that we had let the deceitfulness of money creep into our lives. We knew we needed a change.

In an effort to clearly understand what was missing, we decided to spend a weekend alone at our friends' condo in downtown Atlanta. We needed a change of atmosphere to focus on figuring out our next move. The friends who offered us their condominium agreed to watch our children for the weekend up at our house. A weekend in the suburbs sounded pretty good to them—even with four kids who were not theirs!

While most couples would take a weekend away from their kids to enjoy each other's company, check out the newest trendy restaurant or nightclub, or just blow off a little steam, we chose to do none of those things.

Nope.

Our weekend was devoted to figuring out what it was we wanted to do with the rest of our lives. We went on long walks and shared our deepest thoughts and feelings about life, fulfillment, and our discontent. As we spoke, we both realized that we no longer wanted our lives to be about ourselves. It's hard to imagine that the parents of four young children could possibly feel selfish in any way—but we did. We were always present as parents, but our thoughts rarely extended beyond the white picket fence that surrounded our peaceful and sheltered existence. We had a deep desire to make our lives about something so much bigger than our tiny little bubble we'd been living in.

We talked about all of the friends we'd made over the years and how we each craved deeper relationships than we shared with most of them. I look back on the early years of our marriage when we had very deep, rich relationships. What was different back then? Why didn't we have that now with couples in Atlanta? I think the number-one factor was time or the lack thereof. It takes time to build a friendship and to grow close to people. When we were first married, we had time. Looking back, I can't believe how much time we had! Now, years later, we had four kids, a busy family, and a hectic lifestyle. Free time was a thing of the past.

We often reminisced about the "good ol' days" when life was simple and relationships and time with other couples came easy. We began to realize that we wanted a different version of our old life. We wanted simplicity, deeper relationships, and time.

The other obstacle to forming deep friendships was our willingness to be vulnerable and open with our lives. Jay and I have always been open people who lay everything out on the table. Some people simply don't like that. It makes them uncomfortable to talk about their feelings, mistakes, or marital disagreements. We find it refreshing because—let's face it—we all have struggles. We have never really enjoyed being around people who give the impression that they have it all together. This type of phoniness leads to artificial relationships that never seem to go anywhere.

We had a hard time finding like-minded people we meshed with in Atlanta too. We are very simple, down-to-earth people, and we felt a little out of place living the "big lifestyle." We would go to events and parties and feel like we didn't fit in. Jay doesn't wear penny loafers, and I don't wear designer clothes. We prefer Converse sneakers, Target, and knock-offs.

Often we would find ourselves gravitating to the members of the band performing at the parties. At the time, hearing about their broken marriages and past drug addictions, they were the only ones we could see who seemed real. That was more real to us than trying to keep up with shallow small talk that seemed to inundate the events we attended.

We tried to fit in, wear the right clothes, say the right things, rub shoulders with the right people; but at the end of the day we were empty. We realized that we are really just who we are—simple, average people—and we will never be happy being people we are not.

We were created to be in relationships: first and foremost with God and then with people. Most human beings crave love and desire to be known. Some of us may not admit it, but it's real. We need each other. Although we did not find the depth of relationships we were seeking in Atlanta, I personally found that connection with two close women friends. Jay, however, did not; and that took a toll on him. Yes, we have each other and we are best friends, but sometimes a guy just needs to be with "the guys." They need to play golf, talk about work, and relate on a man-to-man level. I couldn't offer Jay what he could only get from someone who walks in his shoes. He did stay in contact with other close, out-of-town friends, and that seemed to fill the void.

After two days and endless hours of dialogue, we knew there was a higher calling reaching out to us. We wanted to somehow give back for all of the good fortune and blessings God had bestowed upon us. Our decision was to find a mission trip through our church that would give us the opportunity to do something for those in need and the poor.

>> >> >> >> >>

We had both seen images on television with the beautiful and innocent faces of African children in need. Who among us can honestly say those unforgettable photos don't move you or tug at your heartstrings?

Not us!

We can't explain our attraction and the heart we had for Africa other than just knowing in the deepest part of our souls that this was where we wanted to go to be of service. We knew seeing those faces live and in person would make their plight all too real; and, therefore, it would be a life-changing experience. Of course, at the time, we had no way of knowing just how far it would take us away from the only life we had ever known.

When we started looking into mission trip options, the only destination our church was currently offering that allowed families was to China. No offense to China, but we didn't want to go there. Frustrated and unsure of what to do next, we prayed about our desire to serve in Africa until one day, not long after we made the decision to do this type of mission work, we spoke to Jenny Strange. She was one of several people responsible for mission trips at North Point, our church. North Point Community Church is a large church in Alpharetta, Georgia led by Pastor Andy Stanley, the son of Charles Stanley. Andy started this church in 1995 not because Atlanta needed another church, but because he wanted to create a safe place where people who were seeking the truth about Jesus Christ would feel comfortable attending. I think he was successful because North Point now has over twenty thousand people who attend their weekend services.

The missions department decided to open up a trip for families to Africa. The mission was going to be a joint effort between North Point Community Church in Alpharetta, Georgia, and 410 Bridge, an organization that partners people and groups with communities in Kenya.

Perfect!

This was exactly what we hoped to find.

As we continued to discuss the opportunity, Jenny told us she was still looking for someone to actually lead the trip.

"I think you'd be perfect for it," she said, as she and Jay spoke over the phone.

We hadn't thought about the responsibility that comes with leading such a trip, but we also knew God works in very mysterious ways. Everything happens for a reason. If being a leader was what she was asking from us, then who were we to turn her down?

We spent the next six months preparing for our trip. We were headed to a tiny village two hours north of Nairobi called Kiu. When the word spread that there was a missions trip to Africa, several local families reached out to express their interest in participating with us. We had the rare and fortunate opportunity to handpick the people we thought would comprise the very best team. After many hours of meetings and deliberations, we decided on six families who would join us on this journey, with a total of twenty-two of us altogether.

We planned to take our three oldest children—Ben, Bekah, and Abigail—with us. It was difficult to leave Noah, our youngest son, behind;

but he was only four years old at the time, which we felt was too young to make this type of trip.

Working closely with 410 Bridge, we were able to assess exactly what the community we were going to serve wanted from our group so we could work together with the locals when we arrived. We discovered that these types of trips are highly organized. There was a tremendous amount of communication with the village prior to our arrival. After months of dialogue and preparation, the people in Kiu decided that our goal for the ten days we would be there was to build a chicken coop that would house twenty-five hundred chickens.

Undertaking this type of project had several benefits to the locals. First, it would provide a steady source of nourishment. Second, involving the locals meant there would be a common project aimed at getting their troubled youth off the streets. Third, building the chicken coop would provide them with some sort of a business enterprise so they could sell the eggs and, eventually, the chickens.

As the mission trip grew closer, we tried to imagine the journey that was ahead. We counted our blessings for the opportunity we had—not just ours, but also for the experience we were about to give to our children.

When we first signed up for the trip, we thought our group would go to Kiu and help the people with their project in a tangible way while building some new relationships. This experience was the first time we realized the importance of working alongside a community instead of coming in and imposing on them what we think or how we live.

The people from 410 Bridge did an excellent job preparing us for the trip. They gave us a very strict list of dos and don'ts so we didn't make any colossal errors in judgment. They explained to us that no matter how badly we desired to make things better for the people we were about to meet, our mission was to go in and build a chicken coop—working alongside and developing relationships with the African people.

They told us not to give the children shoes because their feet had toughened up from years of surviving barefoot. Once they start to wear shoes, their feet can no longer take the extreme conditions because they soften up. What we would have perceived as doing something to help them would actually hurt them in the long run.

Helping them adjust to our contemporary lifestyle wasn't the reason we were there. Our Western mentality and mindset is to fix things, throw money at the problem until it is no longer of concern, and basically make it all better. It's hard to come up with a solution when we don't necessarily have a full understanding of the problem or their way of life. We quickly discovered that our way of thinking doesn't solve their problems. Long-term change comes with time, perseverance, education, and dedication. The people we were endeavoring to meet had the same drive, initiative, desire, and ultimate goals we did but lacked the resources to facilitate those ideas. Helping provide those resources was the main purpose of our presence in their community.

2 NOTHING, BUT EVERYTHING

JULY 19–31, 2007
KENYA, AFRICA

When we arrived in Africa, our group stayed in Nairobi for the first night; and then we set up camp in Machaco, a village that was two hours from Kiu. We took a bus from Machaco to Kiu, a two-hour trip, every day we were there. The roads, if you can call them that, were more like bumpy, dusty dirt paths. By the time we got to the village each morning, we were already tired and worn out from the grueling commute. We were all struck by the level of poverty we witnessed throughout Kenya, but especially outside Nairobi in the villages we visited. Even the most destitute person in America has so much more than the average African living in these villages.

Despite their poor conditions, we found the African people to be proud, joyful, and fulfilled. Most of the people we came into contact with hadn't bathed in any recent time and wore the same torn clothes every single day, yet they had the biggest, brightest smiles we had ever seen. Their children didn't have Gameboys, Wiis, or iPhones to keep them occupied. They played with an old bucket or crumpled-up garbage they bound together with a piece of rope, which they kicked around like a soccer ball. We saw one little boy rolling an old inner tube along the side of the road as if it was the greatest toy in the world.

There were so many vivid images of the people we met along the way, but none more poignant than the little girl we spotted just standing in a doorway. She had wet herself and the look in her eyes seemed to say, "Does anyone care?" That look seemed to encapsulate the desperation of many of the Africans that we saw. They were trapped in a cycle of poverty with no apparent way to escape. While they had so much joy and community, there was also a deep sense of sadness for the hardship they had to endure. We couldn't get the image of that little girl out of our minds because her eyes and sadness represented how we felt as we saw so many people around us who were struggling just to survive. We felt so powerless to help them.

From the outside, it appeared as if the villagers literally had nothing. How could they possibly be happy living this way? After all, they had no modern conveniences or even the simple and most basic things like a toilet or a bathtub, and still, despite all the things they lacked, there was so much love, peace, and joy coming from them.

We spent our days in the village becoming immersed in and absorbed by their world. Whatever they did, we did. If they were going to collect water, we went right along with them to do the same. Most of us struggled to carry the heavy buckets they hauled around—even the men. Our bodies, no matter how strong or conditioned, weren't used to that type of labor. Certainly none of us on the trip were used to it. Our failings made the locals giggle at us. The African women would easily carry their babies and water buckets *and* balance a giant bag of sand on their back or head without breaking a sweat. They were incredibly strong and resilient. Our respect for them was immense.

We hadn't given it much thought in advance, but it turned out the language barrier was a bit of a stumbling block for us. They spoke Swahili—and we did not. Some of the villagers only spoke their local tribal language, which made it even more challenging for all of us to communicate. A few of the locals spoke English, but when we met someone who didn't, we had to find other ways to communicate. Before we left Atlanta, our oldest son, Ben, thought it would be a good idea to print out a booklet with some useful Swahili phrases. We did our best to learn a few key words and always tried to connect with the locals in any way we could, but it was definitely a daily challenge. Thankfully, we had a wonderful country host, Paul Omondi, who helped bridge the gap. Paul made the most profound impact on us.

Paul was very open as he shared his experiences of growing up in the slums of Nairobi. He told us there was no law enforcement to keep order. The only way the community could fight crime was to take the law into their own hands. Paul was emotional as he told us about watching friends get stoned to death for petty crimes. He witnessed another friend burn to death after the community placed a large rubber tire over his body and lit it on fire.

When we asked Paul about his goals and aspirations, his answer came as something of a surprise to us. He said his dream was to someday become president of Kenya so he could put a stop to the violence and crime and bring an end to the corruption in the government.

Wow.

His passion and desire for change really got to us.

By four o'clock each afternoon, we were back on the bus to make the two-hour drive back to Machaco. We spent the bulk of the ride letting our minds wander from all we had seen earlier in the day. Our thoughts often went to places where we'd think up creative ways to help the village and its people. After a while, though, we'd inevitably realize that our desires might not be their wishes. Just because their living conditions made us uncomfortable, for the most part, the people we met were okay with the way things were. It wasn't our place to try to change their way of life. That was a hard adjustment, especially for a group that was there to make a difference in these people's lives.

By dinnertime each evening, we were all exhausted yet exhilarated from the day's events. Dinner was usually rice or potatoes with chicken or beef tips. It wasn't gourmet, but it hit the spot after a long day.

Each night after dinner, we usually met with the rest of our group to spend a little time debriefing from the day. We talked about our individual experiences, and often the emotions ran pretty high. We discussed the poverty and the horrific living conditions we saw. That dialogue usually led to a discussion on dignity—what it meant and why it was dependent on who God has made each of us to be and not on our judgments. To us, dignity refers to a person's inherent value and worth. Everyone is worthy of esteem and respect because we are made in the image of God.

We spoke of the men we'd met who proudly invited us into their homes, which were often nothing more than mud huts with straw roofs and dirt floors. These men spoke as if their homes were the sprawling mansions we admired from afar throughout the suburbs of Atlanta. Their pride was beautiful. It wasn't about showing off their flashy car or new diamond ring. No, they took pride in simply providing for their families. A roof over their head, a dry place to sleep, and food—albeit minimal— on the table each night. To them, these things were as important as the coveted material collection so many of us spend years acquiring.

By 9:00 p.m., we were all so exhausted we'd literally fall into bed. Our eyes were closed before our heads hit the pillow. The children were especially wiped out at the end of each day. Night passed quickly; and with the breaking morning sun, we couldn't wait to start all over again.

We met a lot of very interesting people during our stay in Africa, but there was one girl in particular none of us will ever forget. On the second day of our journey, we met Teresia, a precious little girl we sponsored as our Compassion International child before our trip. Compassion International is a Christian child advocacy ministry that releases children from spiritual, economic, social, and physical poverty and enables them to become responsible, fulfilled Christian adults. They are a nonprofit organization that provides child sponsorships for more than one million children in twenty-six different countries.

We were so excited to meet Teresia; but at first she was terribly shy, refusing to even look at us when we met face to face for the very first time. She eventually warmed up enough to allow Beth to hug and hold her. Several people peeked in to say hello while we visited together, which eventually became too overwhelming for Teresia. Ruth, the woman who brought her to meet our family, decided to take Teresia outside for a walk so she could calm down. Our daughter Bekah was right there when they made their way out of the office. The two girls had an instant connection. Abigail and Ben were friendly with her, but Bekah stayed by Teresia's side the rest of the day until it was time for her to leave and go back to her village.

BETH» Meeting Teresia was unforgettable for all of us, yet I felt such an instant connection with her once she warmed up. I hugged her and held her close for as long as she would let me. I wanted to spend as much time with her as possible, yet I couldn't help but feel a little torn because I felt like I was letting down the people of Kiu for not being in the village that day to help build the chicken coop. It was bittersweet when Teresia said her good-byes. I wanted to cry but didn't want her to think I was sad for her. I was emotional because I wasn't sure if or when we'd ever see her again.

During my stay in Africa, I met a young woman named Phoebe who was not a part of the village where we were serving but worked there. Phoebe had bright eyes and a confidence about her that, for whatever reason, I wasn't expecting when we met. She was well educated. She had a college degree and a good job working for Compassion International.

Phoebe told me she was making around three hundred dollars a month in wages, half of which she gave to her parents. She shared her family story with me, explaining that her father wasn't able to make enough money to send her brothers to school, so her job was providing for her entire family. As the oldest of four children, and the only one in her family with a career, the responsibility fell on her to pay for her younger brothers' schooling. She didn't mind, as it was culturally a way of life for family to take care of one another.

Unlike many of the other women in the village with whom I shared mostly broken dialogue, Phoebe and I were able to communicate without much struggle, which made a huge difference in the depth and impact of our friendship. She radiated love, kindness, and compassion and shared my deep love for the Lord.

The other women in the village tried to teach me some words in their native tongue, but I had a hard time picking up the language. For the most part, we laughed and just smiled at each other, even though I had no idea what they were saying!

My heart was full from seeing how hard these women worked. They will do manual labor, such as making bricks or carrying manure, and will do that with a baby slung around their backs like it is no big deal. They'd laugh, joke, smile, trust, and open their hearts in a way I had never experienced from other women. Their communication was pure, honest, and lacked any ulterior motives. Being around these remarkable women was refreshing and inspiring all at the same time.

Phoebe and I were able to talk about everything. She couldn't pronounce my name, calling me *Bet* instead of Beth. I loved the way she spoke. She was genuinely honest and real about her life and the struggles she has faced as a young woman living in Africa.

She shared with me how young girls in Africa oftentimes must have sex to earn merely a few pennies. Her willingness to share their story brought to light what the other women in the village simply couldn't put into words. She had no way of knowing just how much I could understand their plight.

As we walked and talked, she opened up to me in a way I hadn't expected. She spoke of the many children in the village who often went days without eating because there wasn't enough food. When I found out how much it would cost to feed fifty kids, I was shocked to learn that it only took eighty-six dollars a month.

How could that be?

How can we live in a world where we have so much while children are going hungry?

I simply couldn't wrap my brain around the thought of a starving child. After hearing that, I gave up my lunch every single day I was in

Kiu, as did many others when they heard about the children too. And still, it seemed so insignificant.

Phoebe's insights helped bring me into their world in ways I simply couldn't imagine. During our time together, Phoebe showed me around numerous houses in the village so I could see firsthand how her people lived.

Phoebe then brought me to her home, which was a tiny one-room structure with a bed and just the basics. Unlike most of the homes we toured in Kiu, Phoebe's place was considered upscale because it had a concrete floor instead of dirt. We had been speaking for a short time when Phoebe turned to give me one of her necklaces. It was the kind that sits right on your collarbone. The colors were bright and full of life.

The gesture caught me off guard because the coordinators of the mission had been very clear to be careful about giving our personal information or items to the people we met throughout our stay. They didn't want us to give out our phone numbers or e-mail addresses; and above all, we were supposed to avoid giving the people we met cash. They explained to us weeks before we made the trip that we would inherently feel the need to do more than we were already there to do. The purpose of the mission was to collectively work together with the people in the village to help them achieve a particular goal. They explained that handouts were frowned upon because they made the villagers dependent and less motivated to do things for themselves. It also made it more challenging on the next group of short-term missionaries because then the same would be expected of them.

While I was well prepared to avoid offering something of my own, no one warned me about receiving such a gracious and lovely gift. I was overcome with emotion by Phoebe's kindness and selflessness. She never once asked me for a thing. She gave me a gift—one that goes far beyond the necklace. It was a beautiful reminder that regardless of the things we have or lack in our lives, at the end of the day, we all have something to give.

Phoebe and I still keep in touch.

She sends me an e-mail or a message on Facebook whenever she makes the two-hour trip to Nairobi. It's amazing to me that even with all of the cultural differences, we can find each other through Facebook!

I really enjoyed getting to know Phoebe and the many other memorable and amazing people we met over the course of the couple of weeks we were in Africa.

JAY» We met so many interesting people in the short time we were in Africa; but I became friends with one particular man whom I will never forget. Sammy is one of the kindest and most thoughtful men I have come across in years. I could tell that his inability to provide for his family had taken a toll on him, yet he still maintained a strong and unshakable spirit. Sammy was generously open with me, sharing his life struggles along with his hopes and dreams. His face and eyes radiated pure joy. He also had a deep faith and positive spirit that was inspiring.

Sammy explained that his inability to earn a decent living had made his family reliant on the community. They were as dependent on each other as they were on God for everything they had. And though he was materially poor and had many needs, he still maintained a positive attitude. He had a strong bond with his wife and children and deep friendships with the members of his community. They shared everything in common. To me, that made him relationally rich.

At first, I thought I only connected with Sammy because he spoke excellent English. He was someone I could talk to and communicate with throughout our trip. But then I discovered that we shared so much in common. We both had incredible and undeniably strong faith, we both had families whom we loved with all of our heart, and we each had a deep and undying love for our wives. Our quick bond took me by surprise because I didn't have a lot of close buddies back in Atlanta. I certainly didn't expect to make this type of connection during our ten-day mission trip. But after experiencing Sammy's positive attitude and heart for God for the first time, I instantly knew we would be friends for life.

I finally got to meet Sammy's wife and kids on the last day we served in Kiu. His wife only spoke a few words of English, but her joy and spirit were also beautiful. Her radiance transcended any language barrier there may have been. She had a huge smile and gave Beth, the kids, and me several warm and sincere hugs. Her body language was so welcoming and loving. There was no need for words after that.

Sammy and his wife were both proud to show us their brick home. It had a dirt floor and no electricity or running water, was dirty, dark, filled with flies, and did not have such a pleasant smell—but it was their home and they were grateful for all they had. My life is fuller for having spent time with Sammy and his family.

It was incredibly rewarding to watch our children throughout the trip too. Our oldest son, Ben, who was thirteen at the time, connected with the local boys who were around his age. Ben is a really fantastic kid. He makes friends everywhere he goes, but the boys he met in Kiu will always share a bond that is hard to define. Our daughters—Bekah, who was ten years old, and Abigail, who was eight—tended to gravitate toward the babies and children. Watching the kids work side by side to accomplish a single goal filled my heart. They worked hard every day and walked away with memories that will last a lifetime.

The experiences we all shared in Africa together as a family were life changing and fulfilling beyond our wildest dreams. We went there uncertain about what to expect. We had no idea the people we met during those two weeks were going to set us on a new path in life. As our two weeks came to a close, we were sad to leave our new friends; but we were ready to head back home and reunite with Noah, think about what we had experienced, seen, heard, and learned, and finally take hot showers and sleep—for days!

3 GOD GIVES EACH OF US A UNIQUE DREAM AND PASSION

God implants a dream into each of us. That dream looks different for every person, but it is definitely there. For some, perhaps the dream is to write a novel, compete in a marathon, or work with disadvantaged kids. Deep down, we all have a dream. But sadly, most people will never act on it.

The changes in the economy have shaken so many people. But we also believe it has awakened them too. People who always thought they'd have a plan B don't. They are discovering the fragility of life and that things can change. People who have spent years living for themselves, obsessed with their accumulated "stuff," are realizing there is more to life than working endless hours only to wake up and do it all over again the next day. Those people have no passion or purpose to their life other than simply making money.

Where's the value in that?

Here's something to consider.

Life is not about what you own.

It's about who you are, what you do, and what contributions you make to others.

Being in Africa gave us a true and new understanding of that and what it means to have a sense of community. The people we met and mingled with for those two weeks really rely on one another. They work together and share everything and don't just think about themselves. They instinctively put others first.

Until we had children, we didn't have to think about anyone else except ourselves. We had lived in an ivory tower for years. We never had to depend on anyone if we wanted something. We always had whatever we needed without depending on our friends, neighbors, or loved ones.

Think about this: when was the last time you asked a neighbor if you could borrow a cup of sugar or give him a hand cleaning out his garage or mowing his lawn?

Here's an even bigger question: how many of you actually know all of your neighbors?

The sense of community and selfless way of life we experienced in Africa was a bit of a culture shock. It was also an awakening for us. Just before leaving Africa we both realized that life, as we knew it, would never be the same. On our last night in Kenya, we both sobbed as we wondered what all of the feelings we were experiencing meant. That's when we thought back to something Paul, our country host, had shared with us—his dream to become the president of Kenya so he could stop violence and corruption in Kenya.

His dream got us thinking about *our* dream.

What *was* our dream?

We had become so caught up in life, having babies, and working hard that we had lost our vision, our focus, and, yes, our dream. We knew for sure that it wasn't the way we were living now.

We both looked at each other but never said a word. We knew we had the same answer.

We wanted more meaning in life.

Our dream was to travel—but not just wander. We wanted to travel with a purpose.

Our dream was *to serve God through our travels.*

We spent the flight home pondering our life.

We envisioned traveling with our family while they are still young so we could give them unforgettable experiences and break them out of the bubble we had all been living in. We wanted to recreate what we had in Africa: purpose, joy, simplicity, and serving. We were definitely lured by the freedom we imagined traveling would bring. We also wanted to be able to see things we had never been able to see ourselves. We loved the idea of being at the ocean or in the mountains, wherever we wanted to be; and then by serving, we would have meaning and purpose in the midst of our travels. It seemed like the perfect answer to our longings. We no longer wanted to be tied down; we wanted meaning to life—but freedom at the same time. We had a vision of having everything that was important to us, right there with us. No more distractions: no yard, house, furniture. We didn't have a big vision; it was really very simple in the beginning. We just wanted to enjoy each other, travel, meet people, serve, and experience all types of people. We thought about all of this and more as we made our journey back to the States.

We flew from Nairobi to Amsterdam to Boston and finally home to Atlanta. It was a long journey that ultimately was just the very start of something much, much bigger than we could embrace or comprehend.

Atlanta was our home; yet once we arrived, it was pretty clear we no longer fit in.

When we walked through the door of what most people would perceive as the perfect American dream, it took only the turn of the key to know for sure that *this* was no longer *our* dream.

How did we get so caught up living this life we never intended?

How did we end up living for all of the things we once saw as necessities but were in actuality total luxuries?

The poverty we witnessed in Africa drove that point home loud and clear.

None of it was making us happy. There was a void in our life that had gone unnoticed for years. And now that we were home, it was the ten thousand–pound elephant in the room we could no longer ignore.

We had awoken the giant. Our dream was on the verge of coming alive.

If we could free ourselves of all of the things we once held so near and dear—if we could loosen the chains that held us so tightly for years, let go of all of this and just walk away—maybe, just maybe, we'd be able to chase that dream down.

Africa had reignited a flame that had been dormant for years. And now that it had been relit, there was no ignoring the beacon of light calling us—make that *screaming* at us—to move toward it.

CHALLENGE #1
God Gives Each of Us a Unique Dream and Passion

» »

We believe that before the creation of time the God of the universe plants a unique dream and passion in each of us. He has given us a unique set of skills and abilities to be used for His glory.

The questions you must answer are: What is your dream? What do you have a passion for? What skills and abilities do you have that you can use to help others?

Our friend Kristi is an Emmy Award-winning television news reporter. For years she worked for KSTP Channel 5, the ABC affiliate in Minneapolis. After being unexpectedly laid off, she was unsure of what she should do next. It wasn't until she went through a class that we teach on serving that she realized her skills and knowledge of the news media could actually be used for good. She has since started a business that trains and equips nonprofits to use the media to promote and connect to their cause. Kristi is an excellent example of someone who has put her passion into action.

How about you?

» What keeps you up at night?
» Has your dream been lying dormant, and now for the first time in years it's whispering to you?
» Will you listen to that whisper and allow your dream to awaken you to use the gifts and passions you have to benefit others?

We challenge you to pursue your dream, identify your passion, and use your God-given talents to serve others.

4 REALITY BITES

AUGUST 1, 2007

BETH» After returning from Africa, we were all tired and weary for days. When we got to the house, Bekah walked through the front door and never made it to her bedroom before falling asleep on the floor in the front room. We spent the next couple of days adjusting and trying to catch up on our chores, mail, and sleep. Jay and the boys cut the grass while the girls and I got everyone unpacked.

As we settled into the comforts of home, none of us could shake the images that would forever be emblazoned on our minds. We had seen poverty at its worst. It was hard to get those images out of our thoughts. We had received permission to take extra duffel bags full of clothing, medical supplies, and soccer balls and give them to the local church in Kiu that was affiliated with 410 Bridge, so they could distribute the goods to those with the most needs. Even though we understood the principles of not giving up our personal goods, it was nearly impossible for us to leave without giving all we could. Our team had all of the clothing we wore throughout the week dry cleaned and then given to the community as well. The feeble effort our team made to bring gifts to their community didn't seem to make a dent. The items we left were a little droplet of water from a sea of excess that we had been living in.

Even our son Ben came back from Africa wondering what all of his stuff was really for. We completely understood his feelings because Jay and I felt the exact same way.

Although we didn't feel guilty for all that we had, we started to regret how we spent the money we made over the years. This realization was hard to ignore. We spent five years acquiring, accumulating, and collecting things we no longer had the need for.

Neither of us expected to look back on our lives with the notion that we had somehow wasted all of these years. We always wanted to live with purpose and intended for our lives to mean something. As we began taking a closer look at things, we couldn't help but wonder what legacy we were creating for our children.

What lessons were we teaching that would shape and mold them to become better adults?

We thought about other powerful families we could look to and asked ourselves how we could be more like them and give of our time and resources so we could touch other people's lives and make a difference.

To be clear—we were not wealthy, at least not by American standards, not by any stretch of the imagination. But we weren't suffering either. The thing is, after we came back from Africa, none of that seemed to matter.

We never imposed the thoughts we were having on our children—and thankfully, we didn't have to. After the experience we shared in Africa, it was obvious to all of us that things had to change.

We knew we wanted to downscale and, with that, maybe even leave the fast-paced lifestyle we had been living in Atlanta. After spending five years there, we never really felt like we ever fit in. We had made several friends but lacked the depth in relationships we wanted to share with others. The area of Atlanta where we lived is lovely, but sometimes it felt like a giant sea of people. We had been kicking around the idea of leaving Atlanta for some time, but it really bubbled to the surface when we returned from Africa.

For us, the choices were limited to traveling the country in an RV, a dream we both shared for years; or moving back to Minneapolis—

something we didn't think was the right answer; but we have extended family there and we had lived there prior to moving to Atlanta, so we pretty much knew what to expect.

We had never taken so much as a family vacation in an RV, let alone set out for an open-ended adventure in one, so the dream was definitely more like a fantasy. The truth is, we truly had no idea what we would be getting ourselves into if we made this our choice. Choosing to live in an RV would be the ultimate if not crazy blind step of faith.

We knew we shared a love for spontaneous adventure and freedom. That's one of the reasons we have a motorcycle. There's nothing like the feeling we get on the open road. The sound of the motorcycle's engine drowns out all of that mind chatter and just lets us be in the moment. It's practically meditative.

We are the kind of people who are willing to try new things. Our motto has always been, *What's the worst thing that can happen?*

This was a huge decision—one we wanted to take our time on and make sure we made the right choice.

We wrestled through our thoughts, fears, and advice from friends and loved ones. We thought about all of the pros and cons for weeks. Since this was a decision that would affect our entire family, we asked the children how they were feeling too.

Ben and Abigail said they were excited about the traveling but weren't altogether thrilled with the idea of not having their own bedrooms if we traveled in an RV.

Bekah made it clear that she *really* didn't want to leave her friends, which we both completely understood.

And Noah?

Well, his biggest concern was leaving behind his toys!

As parents, it is extremely important to us that we didn't talk our children into doing something just because it was what we wanted to do. We were determined not to convince them that our dream had to be their dream too. We have always fostered independence and individuality in our kids. We assured the children that everyone's opinion mattered.

Either we'd all be on board with the idea of traveling the country in an RV or none of us would be. It was an all or nothing proposition.

We kept seeking God to help guide us toward what we should do. We researched options, prayed, questioned, wondered, doubted, and prayed some more. We were leaning toward fulfilling our lifelong dream of traveling with purpose as we were almost certain that it was exactly what God had in mind for our family. Our desire to "someday" make that dream happen was about to become a reality.

Before making our final decision, we decided to take a trip back to Minneapolis. We wanted to see if we would somehow be happier there than we were in Atlanta before fully committing to living on the road. Maybe we were looking for confirmation that the RV was the right choice—or that it was not the answer for our family. So many questions continued to flood our thoughts.

Did we really want to move back to Minneapolis?

Where did we want to raise our children?

What were we *really* looking for?

And would we find that missing piece in Minneapolis?

We looked at houses, scanned various neighborhoods and schools, and realized this was not what we were supposed to do. If we moved back to Minneapolis, we would be swapping one cookie cutter suburban neighborhood for another.

What was the point in that?

The emotional toll of moving and starting all over again was also more than either of us could bear. Neither of us wanted to redecorate another house, find new doctors, join a new church, and start life all over again!

After looking at eleven homes, we were emotionally spent. We decided to go for a bike ride to clear our heads. We rode our bikes across a bridge on the Luce Line Trail, where we came across a bench where we could take a rest. We sat there for a while, barely saying a word.

It was pretty clear that moving back to Minneapolis wasn't the answer we were looking for. We wanted our lives to count, to mean something, to have purpose, and to make a difference in the lives of others. If we were going to jump into our dream to travel the county in an RV, now was the time. And with that final confirmation, our decision was made. We would be what other RV owners refer to as *full-timers*.

We shared the exciting news with our extended family that night. We were all excited and convinced that this was exactly what we were supposed to do. It was exhilarating and scary all at the same time. There was a lot to do before we could effectively turn our dream into a reality. We'd have to sell the house, our extra car, and find an RV and tow vehicle we could afford to buy.

Were we really doing this?

Were we crazy?

It had only been a month since we started talking about the RV. Were we being hasty in our decision?

JAY» Although I grew up going on RV trips with my grandparents, I was very concerned what this trip would mean for my family. I've never been the type of guy who gave much thought about how others saw me; but with this idea, I was absolutely consumed with this change in lifestyle and the effect it would have on our future and what other people would think. I was afraid that buying an RV was nothing more than a depreciating asset. I didn't want to throw away all of the equity we had in our home on something that wouldn't net a return on our investment.

Before we go any further in this story, I have a confession to make.

I am a recovering addict.

I wouldn't have this epiphany until about a year after we left Atlanta, but I think it is important to share so you can fully appreciate where I was coming from and how much this decision touched my life.

The seminal moment came while we were serving lunch to the men in the rehab program at the Redwood Gospel Mission in Santa Rosa, California.

Here's what happened.

I was speaking to one of the guys in the program who was sharing his battle with his addiction to drugs and alcohol. That's when it hit me. My drug of choice was money.

For years Beth and I had struggled financially and had to live very frugally. The pendulum swung the other way when we moved to Atlanta where I began working as a mortgage broker. I started to make money hand over fist.

Once I started raking in the big bucks, I became motivated by my hunger to earn even more. It was like I couldn't stop.

When things were really going well in my business, Beth and I actually sat down and made a list of all of the things we wanted to buy. When we finished compiling our list, there was over forty thousand dollars' worth of stuff!

At the time, I thought about taking a home-equity loan on our house and purchasing everything right there and then. I thought about it for a week or two. Thankfully, I realized taking a loan on our home to pay for stuff we wanted but didn't need was a crazy thought. If we had done that, we would have been saddled with a bunch of debt we wouldn't have been able to get rid of, a second mortgage on our home, and no money to launch our dream. Ironically, we ended up getting almost everything on the list anyway but were able to pay cash for it along the way. There was a lot of satisfaction as we crossed each item off the list. There was also a lot of excess.

My dad never made a lot of money, but he was able to save and invest wisely over the years, which were two traits he passed along to me. When I purchased something, I worked every angle to get the best deal I could; and when it came time to sell, I always expected to get top dollar. With those traits comes the stronghold that money can sometimes have over one's life—as it most definitely had on mine.

Looking back, I now realize I had a lot of fear and control issues when it came to money. I wanted to be financially responsible, to be a good money manager, save whatever we could and pay cash for things so we could live relatively debt free. I don't think there was anything wrong with those ideas, but they began to control all of my decisions. The more I made, the more I wanted. The more I got, the more I had to make. It was a difficult cycle to break.

I began to realize that all the money I had made over the past several years and the things I bought with the money I earned hadn't given me one ounce of happiness. In fact, it ended up adding more stress to my life.

If we were really going to pull the trigger on this journey, I had to change my way of thinking—and fast. Even though I have tremendous faith, it was challenging for me to put my trust in God that He would deliver whatever we needed, especially when it came to our finances. When you can meet your own needs, knowing where your next dollar is coming from is rarely a concern. I wasn't sure I was totally willing to place that in someone else's hands—not even God's.

I could feel God slowly chipping away at my obsession with money. Still, I hadn't completely let go of the freedom or satisfaction I always believed money could buy. In the past, if I needed more money, all I had to do was sell more mortgages. However, that formula dramatically changed when the housing crises hit and dried up my business—which was around the same time we were analyzing our decision to go forward with the RV. The mortgage business was quickly falling apart. The housing crisis all but dried up our main source of income. January had traditionally always been the worst month of the year in the mortgage business, and now October felt like January.

A lot of refining of my ways came when the mortgage market began to crumble. The slowdown in the market gave me lots of extra time to start thinking and reflecting on life and a little less money coming in to spend without discretion.

There was a lot of stress in not knowing where my next paycheck was coming from or how I was going to make ends meet. Working harder wasn't the answer because I couldn't get anyone approved for a loan anyway. The ease in which I made money in the past had given way to financial uncertainty, something I wasn't used to.

In my quietest moments, God began to show me that what I valued and what He valued were very, *very* different. He began to speak to me about letting go of the material things I had held on to so tightly for many years. This was a true awakening for me—one that was there but would take some time to embrace.

It was so amazing to see God show up—especially when I least expected it. Believe me when I say that God is always there.

On the night Beth and I made our decision to pursue the RV, I shared our plan with my dad, someone whose opinion I greatly respect and admire. He quickly voiced his view about losing money and having to buy another home when we got sick and tired of being on the road. Both concerns were valid and something I needed to consider. My brother Kevin also voiced his concerns, which were similar to my dad's. Their opinions mattered a great deal to me—enough that I questioned whether they were right and we were making the wrong call.

I often sought counsel before making any life-changing decisions, oftentimes slowing down to research and seek answers so I know I am doing the right thing. This time, even with the resistance from my family, my mind was made up. I realized that living my life to please others doesn't always lead me down the path of pleasing God, and that was the most important thing to me.

5 GOD WORKS ALL AROUND US

BETH» It was evident that Jay was no longer happy selling mortgages; but if he gave that up, how would he provide for our family? That was one of the questions that kept presenting itself to us over and over again. The other question that seemed to frequently pop up was a universal one in nature but so very personal to us at the time: what *did* we want to do with our lives?

As you can see, we are thinkers. Clearly we didn't enter into this life-altering decision lightly, carelessly, or without lots and lots of thought.

As another way to weed through our worries and clear the cobwebs, we started reading the Bible more closely and taking its words with literal intent. We read together Henry Blackaby's popular Bible study, *Experiencing God*. The thought behind the lesson is that God is working all around us. We just need to join Him in what He's already doing. He doesn't need us to do anything but, rather, chooses to use us. We were both getting the same messages from this lesson, which was a little strange since we hadn't been talking about it or discussing our interpretation of what we had been reading. What we figured out was that God was telling us His plan—and this time...there was no choice but to listen.

It gets back to what Jay said. Although we seek the council of our family and friends, we are ultimately challenged to please God alone. Jay could see it; I could see it. We were to pursue the work God had already begun in our lives, the visions he had already laid before us.

CHALLENGE #2
God Works All around Us

»»

Let's face it, God is big.

He doesn't need your help accomplishing anything. The same God who created the universe, closed the mouths of lions, and opened the Red Sea is working all around you today. He's quite capable on His own; however, He invites you to join Him in the work that He's doing. He wants to display His power through your life. He wants to use your skills and abilities, your talents, even your personality to make an impression on the people you encounter throughout your day. He has a plan for your life.

» Will you quiet yourself, be still, and ask Him to guide you?
» Will you listen to His response and act on what He shows you?

We challenge you to accept His incredible invitation to partner with Him in the work He is doing all around you.

6 FAITH IS THE KEY TO BREAKING THROUGH FEAR

To be totally candid, there were several days of being completely on board with the idea of downsizing and hitting the road; and then the very next day, we'd look at each other and say, "Are we nuts?"

Even though we had made up our minds, we couldn't help but continue to ask ourselves some big and important questions. We were both living in the fear-fueled world of *what ifs*.

What if we ran out of money? The idea of being broke freaked us out. We had always been able to provide for our family, so the thought of not knowing whether or not we could make the money last was overwhelming.

What if we ended up with nothing? What would our family think of us? Would they be disappointed at our decision to go ahead and do this and then sit around saying, "I told you so!"

What if the RV was too close quarters? Would it tear our family apart? After all, we had been used to living in more than ten times the space, so this was a legitimate concern—especially with prepubescent adolescents. We had worked so hard to give our children a stable home life. Were we somehow doing them a disservice by taking them out of that safe and familiar environment and lunging forward into the unknown?

One thing we were certain of is that life is not stable and consistent. Things change.

Maybe our decision would prepare them for real life more than it would hinder them.

We knew they shared our enthusiasm for the adventure. None of us could predict what life would be like on the road.

Would they want to stop midway through?

Would they miss their friends?

How would they adapt to the constant change and transient way of life?

We agreed that each of the children would benefit from this adventure. Still, we had to be absolutely certain we were making the right decision for all of us—and not just ourselves.

We wanted to make sure they would thrive in their new way of life. Were they each strong enough to adapt, or would they eventually crumble under the pressure from the moving around and constant change? We had spent five years building a fairly stable and consistent life in Atlanta. Would we be rocking the boat by implementing this plan? Were we being irrational, foolish, and unwise; or were we creating the greatest opportunity to learn and grow, both as individuals and together as a family?

All of our questions forced us to take a closer look at our family and assess whether or not this type of change would be good for our children.

Our oldest son, Ben, who was thirteen at the time, is an amazing young man. He has always been mature for his age. He never hesitates to offer a helping hand, especially when it comes to caring for his younger brother and sisters. He has become a right-hand man for both of us, and we believed he would continue to be that way on the road. He is incredibly responsible and thoughtful. Whenever we need Ben to jump in, he is always there, which would be a huge comfort going forward.

We also thought Ben would benefit from a trip like this because he needed to come out of his shell a little more than he had in Atlanta. We wanted him to become more comfortable with making new friends, gaining confidence, and taking a risk from time to time. We genuinely thought this journey could bring out those traits in him.

Bekah, who had just turned eleven, is a silly, goofy, and funny young lady who also happens to have a serious and responsible side. She has an interest in cooking and helping around the house, especially in the kitchen. She loves to spend one-on-one time with Beth and loves to help care for her younger siblings. She is very maternal. It sometimes takes her a little bit of time to warm up before she gives in and embraces you like an old pal. She can be more quiet and reserved than her older brother, but she is every bit as confident. She was very comfortable in her little world, but we wondered if she couldn't use a push to come out of her shell. We thought our journey would provide her the opportunity to meet new friends on a consistent basis, and that would require her to get over her shyness, which we believed was a good thing.

Abigail was eight years old. She is a terrifically social girl who makes fast friends with people. She's the thinker in the bunch. She is deeply thoughtful and super intelligent. School comes easily to her, so we didn't have a single worry about Abigail adapting to the road. Abigail loves to keep a journal and jots down elaborate notes on all of her adventures. She feels things on a deeper level than most kids her age. She is sensitive, especially when it comes to the plight of others. We couldn't think of a better way to allow her to make new friends and put her writing skill to use.

Noah had just turned five years old. He is our youngest child and by far the biggest ham in the family. He makes all of us laugh out loud, yet he is a complete and total snuggle bug. He is extremely affectionate, with a tender and sincere heart. If he thinks he has hurt someone's feelings or has done something wrong, his eyes will well up with great big tears. He is so sensitive and thoughtful to other people. He loves to help, always asking, "What can I do for you?" and "How can I pitch in?" He always asks if we are having a good day and offers up many *I love you*s. He is filled with encouragement, sweetness, and kind words for everyone. We had no doubt in our mind that Noah's tenderness would soften people's hearts on the road. We knew he would really impact the people he would meet.

When we started thinking about the gifts and personalities of our kids, all those *what if* questions started fading away. Remembering their God-given strength and compassion reminded us that we needn't let nagging fears overwhelm us and keep us from pursuing our dreams.

When you think about it, what keeps people from turning their dreams into reality?

For most of us it is fear.

Dreams usually die on the table when they are merely in the idea stage. Why?

Because most people would rather let go of their passion than take the risk necessary to see it come to fruition.

A good friend, Gerald Martinez, once told us that faith is spelled R-I-S-K because a true leap of faith is about taking risk. If you never risk anything, you never attain anything. And you can't take risks by living in fear.

When you break it down, faith and fear pretty much have the same definition—a belief in the unknown. Being fearful is a belief in the unknown just as it is when it comes to faith.

People have all sorts of fears, especially when it comes to pursuing their dreams. Perhaps it is fear of failure, the unknown, or rejection that holds you back. Whatever the fear, it acts as a giant hurdle you've got to overcome if you are going to break through.

Whenever we'd let fear seep into our thoughts—and it did, often—we'd try to combat it by asking, "What is the worst thing that could happen?" That singular question has given us the ability to get beyond our fear because the answer usually isn't nearly as bad as we think when we calculate the worst-case scenario.

Despite our plethora of *what if*s, we were still certain that God was telling us to move forward. We had to believe, without a doubt, that He would lead the way, show us where to go, and protect us from making any giant mistakes. Our faith had to overpower our fear or we would never have the courage to break through the barriers that would otherwise have held us back.

Ultimately, we all realized that joy isn't found in treasures here on earth. Its promise is in putting energy, focus, passion, and commitment into hope. Our realization of this kept leading us down the same path. It wasn't so much a significant change in our faith that drove our decision as it was a shift to honor the passion God had given us and deepen our commitment to serve and love Him.

As we slowly began sharing our plan with friends and loved ones, everyone, it seemed, had an opinion. It's true that we had gotten through some hard times. We didn't keep it a secret that Beth had battled with depression in the past. Once she was able to get the proper help through counseling and working with a naturopath who helped balance out her hormones, her life became more balanced and stable. Our friends saw the difference in her and worried that a drastic change might somehow rock our family boat.

When word of our trip got out, people started firing off questions like a fully loaded machine gun.

"What about the kids?"

"What about their friends and stability?"

"What about school?"

School was not especially disconcerting for us since we had pretty much always homeschooled our children. This meant there would be no interruption in their curriculum whether we traveled or not. In fact, the timing of our trip would coincide with Noah starting his studies, which made it a very easy transition for him.

Some asked, "Why don't you rent an RV for a few months and see how it goes?" They thought the thrill and excitement would quickly wear off.

Other friends rallied behind the idea right away, saying they could indeed see us doing this and that our personalities and dynamics were made for this type of lifestyle.

But for a while there, we felt as if we were constantly on the hot seat. The majority of our friends saw our journey as a big step for us, especially our extended families, who didn't quite understand our need or motivation. While Beth's father said he envied us and wished he could have done something like that, Jay's parents questioned the financial validity of our plan. Though in the end, they, too, became supportive. We both wanted to get our parents' approval so we could proceed. For whatever reason, that stamp from each of our folks made all the difference for us.

Before we pulled the final trigger and put the for-sale sign in the front yard, there was one other couple we needed to talk to—Dave and Judy Hill. They had become mentors of ours over the years and, in a way, were like parents to us. We were nervous to tell them what we were considering. We were going to put the for-sale sign in the yard the day they were coming over but decided to wait until after we broke our big news.

When we told Dave and Judy our plan, there was a long pause. There may have even been an audible sigh.

Ugh.

Our hearts sank because we desperately wanted them to be on board as a final confirmation. If they didn't think we were cut out for this, maybe they were seeing something we weren't. That's how important their counsel was to us.

And then they spoke.

"You're made for this. This is exactly what you need to do. Selfishly, we want you to stay here in Atlanta, but we know in our hearts that this is what you're supposed to do."

Hearing that reaction from Dave and Judy was freeing. They were people who knew and understood us. We likely would have stayed our course even if Dave and Judy hadn't agreed with our decision, but it sure felt good to have their support because we valued their wisdom and input.

Deep down, we both knew some people would think we were crazy no matter what, so we were able to accept that without giving it much weight in our decision. Ultimately, we had to get to a place where we didn't care what other people thought—something that would come in due time. We had to learn to be okay if others didn't agree with what we were doing—or worse, we were somehow causing irreparable harm to our kids by taking this trip.

One friend tried making his case by telling us our house is our refuge. Without a home, what would we have? It was a good point. One we needed to think about. After giving it lots of thought, we both realized that a house isn't our refuge, God is. Our house doesn't define who we are. The things we keep inside that house don't define who we are. Our identities are so much more than that. Who we are isn't about what we have or where we live. It's about connections—relationships and love.

That's when we realized that we could be at home and settled no matter where we were because we had God in our hearts and souls.

CHALLENGE #3
Faith Is the Key to Breaking through Fear

»» »» »» »» »» »» »» »» »» »» »» »» »» »» »» »» »» »» »» »»

Fear and faith are roommates. We know from experience that when you exercise your faith and do something that involves considerable risk, you will face fear. David must have experienced fear when he stood before the giant Goliath with five stones and a measly slingshot.

We've come to learn that fear is the head of the dandelion and not the root. The root is unbelief in our hearts. We don't take risks and we cave in to fear because we don't believe that God will do what He says He will. David broke past his fear because he had an unwavering faith and belief that God would empower him to defeat his enemy, Goliath. Before he stepped out on the battlefield, he reminded himself and everyone around him how God had given him the strength in the past as a shepherd to defeat a lion and a bear. What he did next was critically important. He made a declaration. "'This day the LORD will hand you over to me, and I'll strike you down and cut off your head. Today I will give the carcasses of the Philistine army to the birds of the air and the beasts of the earth, and the whole world will know that there is a God in Israel'" (I Samuel 17:46). You know what happened next, what David declared came true that very day. He broke past his fear and took a risk for God because his faith was rooted in his unwavering belief that God would defeat Goliath through him. His declaration was not based on his own power or strength but on the strength of the all-powerful God.

» What fears do you face as you step out in faith?
» Will you remind yourself, as David did, how God has protected and provided for you in the past?
» What declaration will you make?

We challenge you to step out in faith and risk something for God.

7 MEETING MY SOUL MATE

APRIL 13, 1990
KANSAS CITY

JAY» I was working as an admissions counselor at Trinity College in Illinois. My job was to travel around the country meeting prospective students who were interested in our school to try and recruit them. Beth was a transfer student from Kansas City and had called in to speak with a counselor about our school. Thankfully, I was that lucky guy. We had an instant connection and so we began speaking over the phone and writing letters to each other for a month before meeting for the first time on Friday, April 13, 1990.

Yes, it was actually Friday the thirteenth!

It was love at first sight—for both of us. I was smitten from the moment we met. The first night we sat up and talked until four in the morning. Beth shared with me the difficulties she had growing up. I was moved and overwhelmed by her story. Our formative years couldn't have been more opposite. While Beth's past was traumatic, mine was stable.

I grew up on an eighty-acre hobby farm in Minnesota as the youngest of three boys. My parents thought that a place in the country with plenty of land to roam around on would be a great place to raise three boys.

My upbringing was solid.

We had snowmobiles, motorcycles, and even a basketball court in the hay barn. My parents always encouraged us to try new things. I remember them telling me from an early age that I could be anything that I wanted to be. They allowed each of us to pursue what we were interested in and then supported us in every endeavor we pursued.

I was always super competitive. Still am. I started skating when I was five years old; and while hockey was my main sport, I also played basketball and soccer. My brothers and I had a tradition of playing football together on Sunday afternoons in the backyard after watching the Vikings play on television. To this day, I'm still a hopeless Vikings fan. When we weren't playing football, my brother Kevin and I were playing golf or tennis. One time, after watching the Wimbledon Tennis Tournament on TV, we cut the grass extremely short on the side of the house, used our volleyball net as a makeshift tennis net, and played some hard-core tennis. It worked great with the exception of the ball going in random directions from hitting the huge earthworms that buried themselves in our yard. Every free second I had was steeped in competition of one form or another.

While I loved sports, I found a new passion in fifth grade when I realized I could sing. I started doing solos at the church we attended; and once I was in high school, I traveled around the country where I sang at music competitions sponsored by our church. I attended a Christian high school that was located in the basement of our small church in Delano, Minnesota. There were only forty kids in the whole school. The year I graduated, I was the only senior. I have to admit, it was pretty awkward being the only one walking down the aisle to "Pomp and Circumstance." The standing joke to this day is that not only was I voted most likely to succeed and fail, but I was also the homecoming king and queen.

While I grew up in a Christian home, it was during the summer of my sophomore year at Northwestern College that I made my faith my own. I was living in Dublin, Ireland, working with Greater Europe Mission. I began reading the Bible to see what it had to say on my own instead of relying on what my parents had taught me to believe. I came to some strong convictions and decisions during that summer.

While I was raised with strong values and morals, it was during my time in Ireland that I made a conscious decision to save myself for marriage.

After meeting Beth, I fell head over heels in love. We spent a month talking over the phone, which built a great foundation for our relationship. Things got serious fast when Beth made the decision to move to Chicago to work as a nanny so we could live near each other. We spent every spare moment we had together. We loved talking and hanging out. We had our share of issues, but we quickly became best friends and fell madly in love.

From the beginning, Beth and I talked about the importance of staying pure in our relationship. However, the more time we spent together, the bigger the challenge we were having keeping to that promise. We didn't seek people out who could hold us accountable to our pledge to stay pure—something I look back on with regret. One night we stayed up too late together. My feelings came on quick and without regard for a boundary that should have been in place. I should have been stronger and more in control, but we placed ourselves in a tempting situation. I wanted to be with Beth in every way. I gave in to the temptation without regard for the promise I had made to myself and to God.

I felt horribly guilty about what happened. I had been immoral; and for me, that was devastating. I thought my life was over because of the way I was raised and my strong convictions in this area. I felt like I needed to confess what I had done, so I decided to tell my boss about what happened because I had a sincere desire for help and accountability. I looked up to my boss. I thought of him as a father figure. I was certain he would guide me toward doing the right thing, hold me accountable, and, at the same time, help alleviate some of my guilt.

When I told him about what had happened he didn't say a word for what felt like an eternity.

"You know, my wife and I struggled when we were dating…but not like that," he said, staring me down as if I had committed the worst possible sin.

I felt completely and totally rejected. Here I was, opening up and asking for help—even saying I didn't want to keep sinning and he was judging me.

To add insult to injury, Beth and I actually worried she might be pregnant, a concern I also shared with my boss that day. We were so young, dumb, and naïve. I think I actually believed he would find compassion in his heart. Instead, he fired me.

About a week after my confession, my boss came to see me with the head of Human Resources—never a good sign. They handed me a box for my personal belongings, asked for the keys to my company car, and told me I was fired. Just like that.

Looking back, I would have fired me too. I had an inappropriate relationship with a prospective student. I'd say that's cause for dismissal. But at the time, I was devastated and confused.

Unemployed and in need of money, I took the first job I could find working at a place called the Holiday Shop. It was the middle of July, ninety degrees outside, and I was selling Dickens Villages and Christmas ornaments. To this day, I cringe whenever I hear Mannheim Steamroller because they played their holiday CD over and over all day long.

BETH» When I met Jay, I had been a Christian for about a year or so. I had just gotten out of a serious relationship about eight months prior and honestly was not looking. In fact, I was quite content being alone— just God and me. I thought my checkered past was behind me. I knew my past choices and mistakes had been forgiven, and I believed that they could no longer affect me. Little did I know that the pain and emotions were lurking under the surface like a big fat beach ball being held under the water, waiting to rush to the surface as soon as the pressure gave way.

Jay and I fell madly in love with each other rather quickly, but unfortunately we had issues right from the start.

Okay, to be totally honest, they were my issues that became his problem when we got together.

I grew up in Kansas City as the youngest of six children. We all struggled as we watched my mother battle with her depression over the years. She spent much of my young life struggling with mental instability and even going in and out of mental institutions. We never knew how she would be from one day to the next. And then, one day, my mother hung herself. I was just five years old. I didn't understand what happened, nor could I possibly recognize the impact and the severity my loss would ultimately have later in life.

After my mother's suicide, I grew up with a huge void in my life. I went from one day having a mother to her just suddenly being gone. And as strange as it may sound, I actually spent many years feeling guilty about her death. I often asked myself if somehow I was the straw that broke the camel's back. Maybe it became too much for her when I, her sixth and last child, was born. I know now that this is not true, that my mother loved me dearly; but as a young, confused, and abandoned little girl—the feelings were very real.

Everything in our home became chaotic and unstable after my mom's death. My father wasn't used to running the household, so we rarely had enough food in our refrigerator to feed our family. Often I would go to the neighbor's house and ask for a sandwich to help fight off the severe hunger pains.

My father also spent most of his time at the local bar. I don't recall seeing him much. I realize now that he was trying to cope with the overwhelming loss and the huge responsibility that was before him—raising six kids alone.

I don't recall having a lot of conversations with my dad back then. When he finished his dinner, he'd retreat to his bedroom and watch TV behind a closed door until he would eventually fall asleep.

Looking back, I believe my father withdrew because he carried so much pain. He had lost his wife and best friend...and there was nothing he could do to get her back. I believe he also struggled with guilt, a battle that seems to plague all family members and close friends of suicide victims. You are left to wonder if you could have done something to prevent it from happening. My father was tormented with thoughts like that. I can only guess that there must also be some kind of shame associated with your wife taking her own life. Although my mother was very sick, my dad felt some responsibility for her death. My dad was a good man, and he tried his hardest to be there for us, but the pain and regret he lived with were too overwhelming.

My older siblings each found their own way to spend as little time at home as they could after Mom died. Since my father wasn't around to supervise me, I pretty much did whatever I wanted to do. I skipped school, had the run of the neighborhood, and rarely ever bathed. Shortly after my mother passed away I was a victim of sexual abuse from someone I knew. It started right after we moved from our house to a three-bedroom apartment. I was shocked and devastated but too afraid to tell anyone. I remember one boy saying, "Your body is not your own. It is mine and I can do whatever I want with it."

My innocence was stolen from me, and it wasn't long before I lost all self-esteem and self-respect. I was so young when this started to happen that I grew up having no understanding of what personal boundaries were. I grew up believing that I wasn't my own person. I was brainwashed by these destructive lies and accepted them as truth.

I didn't have a parent who was present enough to protect me or tell me otherwise, so why would I think anything differently?

There were no rules, no boundaries, and no one was watching out for me. I had no one I could turn to and talk about how I was feeling or about the terrible things that were being done.

Once I saw myself as worthless, it was easy for others to see me that way too. Even adults began to take advantage of my vulnerability. I felt guilty for allowing all of the abuse to happen—so much so, I chose to never utter a word about my shame and embarrassment.

In a way, it was my own coping mechanism for the life I was living. I was terrified that I would upset someone if I spoke out and they'd become angry with me, so I chose to stay helplessly silent to avoid that type of confrontation.

The abuse continued for five years. The person who was assaulting me finally stopped when my father got remarried. Although I was relieved it was over, the emotional damage had already been done. At the age of ten, I was filled with hatred and anger.

My stepmother had five children of her own, so altogether (including a foster sister who joined our family when I was a little girl) there were twelve children in our new family. Within our new blended family, there were eight of us still living at home.

When my father shared the news that he was getting married, I was thrilled at the prospect of having a new mom. I had dreamed of someday having someone I could share my feelings with and who would love and protect me. As a little girl, having experienced such intense heartache in my short ten years of life, I was overly sensitive and oftentimes weepy and emotional. I craved warmth and affection. Unfortunately, my stepmother, by personality, was nothing like that. She was very strict and dominant, having herself grown up in a very large, ironclad Irish Catholic family that showed little emotion. In some ways, I believe she was as unprepared for us as we were for her. Our two families were worlds apart, and we struggled to mesh together as one.

Had my stepmom known about the abuse I had been through, our relationship possibly would have been different; however, I couldn't bring myself to speak a word to her. In her eyes, she was dealing with a rebellious and unruly teen who was railing against her authority. Although she tried to manage as a good mother, I had spent five years without any parental guidance, structure, or discipline. So I never felt the need to comply with her demands and rules. I wasn't all that interested in someone telling me what to do—and boy, did I show it.

I began to rebel—big time. I swore at her, told her I hated her, and refused to let her win a single battle. The harder I rebelled, the harder she came down on me.

She tried the best she knew how to reach me and show love to me, but my eyes only saw rejection. Her rigidity and harsh nature spelled displeasure to me. I pushed away and isolated myself.

Outside the home in grade school, I wore the shame of my life and became extremely introverted. I was teased relentlessly and withdrew even further. I tried my hardest to stay under the radar and just blend in, but that was easier said than done.

Later, when I started high school, I made the decision to never tell anyone about the struggles I had at home. No one knew about the sexual abuse or that my mother committed suicide. I wanted to keep my dark secrets as far away as I possibly could from my new friends, teachers, and life. My goal was to self-protect so that people would accept me without judgment or pity.

I desperately wanted to fit in as a way of fulfilling my deep yearning to be loved through the affection of others. I wanted to be popular and was eager to become friends with everyone. This is when I began to live a double life. I learned how to separate myself from my family and the pain and chaos of my home life and my poor choices and go to school playing the part of a "normal" teenage girl.

As my first year in high school progressed, I did whatever I could to disassociate myself from my family life. I came home as little as possible. When I finished volleyball practice or games, I'd go to friends' homes, practically living there without anyone catching on—their parents or mine.

The older I got, the worse the confrontations at home began to get. The second my stepmom tried to discipline me, I'd explode. I was a ticking time bomb waiting to go off at any moment. Our arguments would become volatile and contentious, anger going in both directions—it had become traumatic for everyone.

I spent from ages ten to eighteen in complete discord. I began having waking blackouts, which I would later realize was my way of coping with what was happening. The blackouts were a strange half-sleep state that I hated when they came on. I could feel darkness seep inside my body, which I would fight until I simply had nothing left before it took over. I could hear everything going on around me but was somehow able to remove my emotional connection. It was as if I was no longer a part of what I was experiencing. I never knew where or when these blackouts would occur, but being around my family seemed to trigger them.

Then one day it hit me: I didn't have to live like this. I didn't have to live a life where every day is a fight for survival. So the summer before my senior year, I quickly and quietly packed my bags and ran away to Texas. I had been working at a local thrift shop. My boss knew how miserable I was at home and offered to pay for my flight. And as my naïvety had landed me into trouble many times before, I once again found myself in a position that I didn't expect to be in. While I innocently thought he was just being nice, he had ulterior motives. Thankfully I was able to escape his clutches and keep myself around a group of people I had met to stay safe. After two weeks, somehow my parents found me and demanded that I come home. I angrily and reluctantly moved back. To be honest, the only reason I complied was because I was unable to transfer my school records without parental consent, and I didn't want to add dropout to my already colorful life résumé.

By the time I was a teenager, I actually became very comfortable living a double life. I'd go to school during the day pretending to be a perfect Catholic schoolgirl and then continued stealing, drinking, staying out late, and getting punished all the time for my uncontrollable behavior. The dichotomy was numbing, and it was how I chose to deal with my experiences and the painful emotions that came from them. I eventually lived in that numbness for years to come.

My life continued to spiral downward as I began seeing a married man. I hid this from everyone, yet somehow my parents found out. My dad made an attempt to take me out to dinner to confront me and get involved in my life, but it was too late. I was so deeply mired in sin that I couldn't imagine a way out. I crafted a pretty good lie to get him off my back and then got through the rest of dinner without any more discussion on the matter. I could tell my dad was making a good attempt to reach me and pull me out of my self-destructive life, but I was too numb and scathed.

My self-hatred had grown so intense that I often found myself sitting on the kitchen floor with a knife to my wrist, crying and desperately wanting to end the intense pain. I was petrified to actually go through with it for fear of doing irreparable damage instead of killing myself.

The pain became too much to bear and I could no longer live with it, but I didn't want to end up like my mother either. It was during one of those helpless nights as a teenager that I started to understand a little bit about the pain my mother must have felt to take her own life.

After high school all of my friends went away to college, and I stayed home and kept on living a destructive lifestyle—numbing myself to survive. I was devastated and mortified at who I had become and felt trapped in my life. I was making one bad choice after another. By the time I was eighteen years old, I had a string of unhealthy relationships, was stealing, drinking, lying, and fighting all the time. I could see what was happening to me, but I didn't care about the outcome.

I often wondered what it would take for me to bottom out. I wasn't all that interested in sticking around long enough to find out.

I was sick of my life and decided I had had enough. I packed my bags and moved to New York to work as a nanny for a military family that I had met through my brother-in-law, who was also in the military and was a teacher at West Point. It was my last-ditch effort to distance myself from the hardships I faced growing up. I never wanted to speak to my family again. All I wanted was a fresh start.

Thankfully, my oldest sister, who was twelve years older than I and who had been removed from the drama at home, was living there with her husband and three children. Although I lived with the family I was a nanny for, I found comfort in hanging out at my sister's house, helping her with her kids, and experiencing life with her. She was the oldest in our family and had become somewhat of a mother figure in my life. Even though she had gone through trauma herself, being the one who found my mom, she had a loving husband and a stable life. She was a beacon of hope to me.

Although I had gotten away and was trying to start a new life, I discovered a difficult truth: anytime you move, you always bring yourself with you…and sometimes that's the root of the very problem you are trying to escape.

I quietly continued to battle low self-esteem and a host of other issues, including my newfound one—bulimia.

For the first time in my life, I found myself putting on weight; and since I had never had to diet, I didn't know what to do. I began to starve myself for days, usually having only a diet soda or half a bag of popcorn. My hunger would become so intense that I would go to the nearest grocery store and frantically grab cookies and peanut butter off the shelf. I would shove them down quickly, not letting the guilt stop me. In fact, the guilt was what pushed me to eat more. I felt so much shame and remorse; and the lower I sank, the more the gluttony turned into a type of self-abuse. I would then go and "get rid" of my food, or so I thought; but ironically the number on the scale continued to go up. Before I knew it, I was trapped in this binge-purge cycle—sometimes purging three to four times a day. No one knew. Once again, I found myself in a place of total shame and embarrassment, and I chose to withdraw.

Shortly after arriving in New York, I met a guy who was very different from the boys I knew back home. He was a kind, loving, and compassionate guy who wanted nothing from me. I didn't feel obligated or indebted to do things I didn't want to do, and that was unusual. I knew he really cared about me as a person and not just what I could give him. I didn't know how to behave around him; and I was terrified that once he knew my past, he would toss me to the curb. He began to bring me around his friends, who were all so nice to me. I didn't understand what made them so different from other people I had met over the years, but there was a definite difference in how these people treated me.

We started spending a lot of time together without him having any expectations or creepy demands. He used to tease me about my sailor mouth. It's true—I used pretty salty language on a regular basis when I was younger. He told me it didn't sound right coming from a girl.

We also started attending church and Bible study classes on a regular basis, something I hadn't done before we met. Although I was raised as a Catholic, I skipped church as often as possible. I believed in God and the seven sacraments—all that I was taught in school—but I had never given much thought to the meaning or significance of those teachings. My friend's pastor told me he had previously been in the Catholic church, so he seemed like the logical person to talk to about my beliefs. I was so taken aback by the faith of my new friends that I fired off question after question at him, trying to understand the teachings of the Bible.

I had never opened a Bible let alone read it. I didn't even know people could read it on their own without being in church. To me, it was a big dusty book that sat on the coffee table that no one ever touched. God was distant for me. I believed that He had abandoned me like my mother, that He was aloof like my father, or that He was a God that only cared about rules. And since I could never measure up, He was continually displeased with me. I associated God with my family—that is until I spoke to my friend's pastor.

He spoke of a different God. He talked about a God full of love and compassion, who created me in His image, a God who knows me and loves me, who sent His Son to die for me.

This was huge news.

I knew this was the same God that my family believed in; however, this was the first time I had ever heard that He wanted a relationship with me. That He was not concerned with whether I followed all the rules, performed enough good works, went to church every Sunday, consistently went to confession, or said the right prayers. I learned for the first time that I can't earn God's love or work my way to heaven. His mercy is freely given through the sacrifice of Jesus.

What a relief! I no longer had to try to measure up. The truth is, I never will. None of us can. Being "good enough" is a vain attempt that we were never meant to reach.

In the Old Testament God required sacrifice and rituals for sins, but when He sent His own Son to die on the cross, Jesus became the sacrifice once and for all—for each of our sins. Jesus was sent to bridge the gap between God's holiness and our sinfulness. He became the sin offering, which brings forgiveness, restoration, and eternal life.

Knowing this truth about God was eye opening, but believing something as fact and actually receiving it as a personal gift are two different things. I had believed in God, yes; but I never realized that, like any gift, you have to receive it and discover it as your very own. Having a relationship meant that He wanted all of me, but He would not barge into my life; instead He would wait to be accepted. He gives us each a free will—we get to choose what we do with it.

The pastor told me that if I wanted to receive the gift of Jesus into my life all I had to do was acknowledge my need for a Savior and confess my sin through a simple prayer, inviting Him to come into my life and have complete control, and He would do the rest.

I didn't understand all that was being shared with me that day; but I realized the void in my life could never be filled with alcohol, men, food, or any person. I had tried it all and was still empty and hopeless. I needed and wanted something more powerful and life-giving.

I was enormously moved by my conversation with the pastor. So much so that a few nights later, I got down on my knees in my bedroom and cried out, "I give up, God! I need You, and I beg You to come into my life and take over. I've made a complete mess out of it, but I give it to You. I know I've sinned against You and I'm sorry. Please forgive me. Please come in and change my life."

It was at that exact moment that I felt His presence for the very first time. It was as if that darkness I'd been carrying with me since my mother died simply vaporized.

Poof.

Gone.

A week later, for reasons I still don't totally understand, I called my stepmother to tell her I loved her. And the truth is, I did.

She attributed my change of heart to leaving home and growing up. She figured that most kids go through their teenage rebellious years but eventually come around. But that isn't what happened. I wanted to tell her the truth and share with her the marvelous awakening I'd had, but I didn't. My family had been exposed to religious fanatics before, and I wanted to prove this wasn't some "spiritual high." This was God changing my life. I just wanted to love and forgive her without a lot of explanation. I was at peace for the first time in my life—and I liked how that felt.

My relationship with my dad also changed. Through many conversations, he admitted to not being there for us as we went through the loss of my mother. He was always quick to apologize and acknowledge that he was wrong, which I deeply respected. This led to forgiveness and a close and loving relationship between us. What I was faced with, however, was forgiving those in my past who would neither acknowledge their sin nor apologize for it. I had to forgive them because God's Word tells me to, regardless of whether they deserved it. I also had to forgive myself, which was the most difficult. I had regret over making many wrong choices in my life, and I needed to quit punishing myself and accept the forgiveness God had given me.

I continued dating the guy who brought me to church, but I soon learned that he had a very high standard for his future wife. For one, she had to be a virgin, which I clearly was not. I hid my past from him, rationalizing that maybe once he got to know me, he could look past this and love me in spite of my "scarlet letter." In an effort to keep him from discovering the real me, one lie led to a thousand others and before I knew it our whole relationship was based on falsehood. I had lied so much in the past that I was actually quite skilled at it. I was able to convince him that I was the woman of his dreams, and we soon became engaged.

However, I was a Christian now. Suddenly, living a life of lies and cover-ups no longer felt like second nature. It was repulsive and uncomfortable. I knew I had to tell him, but how? Before I had the chance, he broke off the engagement with no explanation whatsoever.

I was heartbroken—for the first time.

Despite the deception, I had never had my heart come alive so much in a relationship. I knew it was because God was at the center, and He was chipping away at the hardened layers of my heart and was beginning to allow me to open myself up to love and be loved by others.

About six months after breaking up, I moved back to Kansas City with the intention of going back to school. I moved back into my parents' home temporarily while I looked into nearby colleges.

I was beginning to see how forgiveness was changing my relationships. Living at home, I now enjoyed the time to reconnect with my parents, and I also began to see them with new understanding.

I enrolled at the local junior college but continued to pursue going to a nearby Christian college. One school I was applying to was Trinity College in Deerfield, Illinois. I called the school and was transferred to Jay, one of the admissions counselors. We immediately hit it off and talked for longer than the typical exchange that would normally take place between a counselor and a student. We agreed to talk again later that night. Each conversation we had led us deeper into what became more than a counselor-student relationship. This was not my intention at all as I was not interested, nor was I looking for a relationship.

Jay was working in Chicago and I was living in Kansas City, which meant that we spent the first month of our relationship talking over the phone. We devoted countless hours to talking and getting to know each other. Then, on April 13, 1990, he flew to Kansas City to meet me. Although we felt like we had become so familiar with each other, it was our first real face-to-face date. That first night we sat on my couch talking, and I knew I had to share my story with him. I could no longer live a life of lies, and I believed that if Jay and I were meant to be together, he would be able to accept the truth of my past. If he couldn't, then he wasn't for me—plain and simple.

I'll never forget his response when I told him about my past. He said, "I believe that God has done an incredible thing in your life. That's not something to worry about hiding, and it's not something that might scare me away. It's something to celebrate and perhaps share with others who are struggling. You turned your life around with God's help; and to me, that's nothing short of amazing."

Jay and I fell head over heels for each other. I took a nanny job in Chicago to be near him because neither of us wanted to date long distance.

We became close in our relationship, too close, and it was as devastating for me as it was for Jay. After committing my life to God, I made a decision not to give myself away to anyone else until marriage. I even had a couple of boyfriends before Jay who wanted to take things too far, but I wouldn't let them. It was a firm decision and I had planned to stick to it.

It surprised me when I became so overcome with passion and love for Jay that I actually went back on that precious promise I made to myself. Every sexual act in my past had not been out of love, but rather to find love. My relationship with Jay was different, and I wasn't prepared for the emotions, feelings, and longings that welled up inside of me to be as close to him as possible.

I regretted our decision to become intimate immediately afterwards and profusely beat myself up over the mistake we had made. Of course, with my tainted past, I felt responsible. I felt that I corrupted Jay and led him into it. However, I now realize that was not true. We both made the mistake together and suffered the consequences of it together, as it seemed to rip away at the foundation of our relationship.

No one had ever shared the truth with me about the damage premarital sex can do in a relationship. It's typically glamorized and thought of as a necessary element of growing closer. However, for us, it brought confusion and broke down trust, respect, and friendship.

Our passion for each other quickly turned sour as the first wave of fighting broke out. Jay had a way of getting under my skin. He grew up in a family where practical jokes and teasing were a part of their family life. He pushed my buttons, sometimes going too far without really meaning it. I'd get so angry that I would physically lash out in uncontrollable anger. I'd throw things, scream, hit, and even attempted to jump from his car as he drove down the highway.

This became a regular occurrence in our relationship whenever Jay and I got into a disagreement. My temper would flare up, then I would be so ashamed and would apologize profusely; and to make up for it, I would work overtime at being the best girlfriend I could be. Even though I had found peace and serenity in my love for God, I hadn't quite worked out my inability to control my emotions. Something would get triggered in me whenever Jay and I would fight that brought up all of my old patterns and behaviors.

Still, Jay was remarkably understanding and patient. All he wanted to do was love me. Even when I'd throw my engagement ring at him, he'd stay calm and nonreactive.

"We'll work through this," he'd say.

We both knew my behavior was not normal and that something wasn't right; but Jay continued to love me, sticking with me in spite of our mistakes and how often I tried to push him away. I still wasn't sure I deserved his or anyone's unconditional love, and maybe in some way I was trying to prove it through my uncontrollable behavior.

The extreme ups and downs in our relationship continued throughout the year that we dated and until we got married, about a year and five months after we met. Despite the roller-coaster ride of emotions and the fact that I continued to wrestle with unresolved anger despite my newfound faith, we knew we were meant to be together. I was thankful for Jay's tenacity, commitment, love for God, and undying love for me. Another bonus was his sense of humor. He sure knew how to lighten things up. Sometimes when we would get into an argument, he would ask me if he needed to get his hockey helmet on. I couldn't help but break into laughter. There was some truth to that, which was sad to admit.

Another quality I later came to appreciate about Jay was his ability to communicate and work through conflict. He had grown up in a healthy home where they talked out their differences without letting things escalate. I, however, responded to conflict by either clamming up and giving Jay the silent treatment or blowing a gasket. There was no in-between. Thankfully, Jay was persistent and held firm to his commitment to never let the sun go down on our anger. He would stay up all hours to talk through our arguments in a civil manner. At times, I despised this because it forced me to tread in unfamiliar waters; but I came to love and appreciate his determination because, in the end, it resulted in a deep connection and closeness that I had never experienced before.

I continued to dig into my Bible daily, and my relationship with Jesus was my source of strength and hope, but all the while I struggled to manage the intense feeling that something wasn't right inside my body. I loved my husband immensely, poured my heart and soul into being a mother to my young children, and delighted in my role as a homemaker. I felt fulfilled in my life, yet there were undeniably dark emotions lurking under the surface that would continually shove their way into my thoughts and beliefs. I felt hopelessly trapped in a life of managing my emotions and never really being free to experience all the joys God had given me.

Life flew by at breakneck speed. In under eight years, we had three children, had moved three times, and Jay had four job changes. After our third child, Abigail, was born, I began struggling with what I thought was postpartum depression.

I used to have this low sensitivity for people who said they were depressed or anxious because I always felt like they were using these generally accepted terms as a crutch for whatever the real issues were in their lives. I'd often point out how much we have to be thankful for, with total disregard for how they were really feeling. I had this "look on the bright side" attitude. If you've never lived in a state of depression, it is extremely difficult to understand what it feels like or to truly be in touch with it.

And then, you suddenly find yourself smack in the middle of a depression yourself—one you didn't see coming and weren't prepared for in any way. That's what happened to me.

I was determined to pull myself up by my bootstraps; but no matter how hard I tried to outrun, outsmart, or ignore my sadness, there it was. I turned to God and daily begged Him to remove the dark cloud, but no amount of praying or Bible memorization took away the crushing hopelessness that became part of my daily existence.

From the outside looking in, during the early years of our marriage and when our children were young in Minnesota, Jay and I seemed the picture-perfect Christian family. We were involved in our church, where Jay sang and led worship on the weekends and at our midweek service. We led a small group Bible study, and people in our community looked at us as the model family. But behind closed doors, my world was slowly unraveling.

Jay was in full-time ministry and was on a personal mission to bring people closer to God. He was in the midst of starting a church with a group of others in Minneapolis for twentysomething singles and college students. His role was overseeing the communication team, all of the ministries, and their leaders, along with leading worship. He was often out very late at night, handing out fliers to kids after concerts, hoping they might be searching for something more and would possibly come to our church to see what it was all about. In a way, ministry had become Jay's mistress.

I was busy at home trying to play the picture-perfect wife and mother, taking care of three small children, doing all of the housework, and cooking without a single complaint. I knew Jay was busy doing "God's work," and I truly thought that I could best support him by making sure everything was running smoothly at home and not speaking a word about my inner struggles. I tried my best to hold this enormous beach ball of emotions under the water; but at times it would thrust through the surface, and I would again react in extreme ways. My fits of rage were drastic and unpredictable, and I was continually apologizing for and excusing my behavior.

I felt a host of conflicting emotions. Deep inside, I felt neglected by Jay. It seemed that the kids and I played second fiddle to his passion to change others' lives. He worked so hard and would come home with little left to give. I tried to understand but silently wondered how much we really mattered to him.

There were other days that my emotions would bounce in the other direction and I would reflect on the depth of my dysfunction, and I felt thankful that Jay was the man that he was. How could I complain when I had a husband who loved God with all of his heart and who was doing all he knew how to love us and serve others wholeheartedly? I felt incredibly blessed and wondered at times if Jay regretted marrying me.

Then one day the pressure gave way and I sat Jay down to tell him the scope of how I felt.

"I either want a divorce, or I want to kill myself," I said as tears streamed down both cheeks. I literally could not decide which was the better option. I can only imagine those words are not fun to hear because they were terribly bitter to speak.

I don't think Jay ever saw those two choices coming. I had become so good at pretending my entire life; and although I had my moments of erratic behavior, I was still able to act as if everything was just fine—when, in fact, I was an unraveling disaster.

Once the truth was out in the open and I no longer had to keep up the facade, it didn't take long for me to slip into a full-blown depression. I slept until noon every day and was physically unable to take care of the kids. Jay had to cut back on his hours at work to be home to care for the children and me.

Jay and I sought advice as to how to deal with the depression. One pastor, who did not believe in medication or counseling, suggested that the past was behind us and that I needed to keep pressing on and walking forward in truth and forgiveness—and that by practicing thankfulness, the depression would leave me. The problem was, I had been trying that for years. I felt that I was now getting a taste of what it was like to be on the other end of someone giving you pie-in-the-sky advice when they have never walked in your shoes. I knew he meant well, but both Jay and I felt that I needed a different type of help.

Another one of our pastors, who had previously been in the medical field, saw that I was drowning emotionally and suggested that I needed a life vest. He knew that medication would get my head above water so that I could begin to deal with the issues in my life. We agreed.

I began seeing a counselor, which immediately seemed to help. It was nice to have someone to talk openly to without worrying about judgment or criticism. I found some help but continued to feel like I needed something more.

I then scheduled an appointment with a medical doctor. My first visit was with an extremely impatient doctor who hastily diagnosed me as bipolar, primarily after hearing about my mom's history. He prescribed two and then eventually three different medications, one being an antipsychotic drug. I had no idea. We later found out that this same doctor was giving this diagnosis to many of his patients, and he later ended up suspiciously leaving town.

The drugs seemed to make matters worse. I felt numb and detached from the world around me. I would regularly have disorienting experiences where I could see life going on around me, but I was no longer a part of it. I was not myself and withdrew even further. I made several more visits to the doctor to have my medication adjusted, but we could never get it just right.

I began to sink deeper into hopelessness, wondering if I'd ever live a normal life.

One night after a heated discussion over the phone, I decided to soak in a hot bath to give my emotions time to cool down. We lived in an old home in Minneapolis where the doors were made of heavy, solid wood with a deadbolt lock. The kids had gone to bed, but I automatically locked the door, not wanting to be bothered. I ran a hot bath and slipped myself into the water.

I was not in my right mind as the medication seemed to confuse my thoughts. I felt helpless against the overwhelming feeling that I was damaging my kids and that my family would be better off without me.

Thoughts of suicide had been plaguing me since my childhood, and I had become skilled at listening to them and fantasizing about following them through.

This time was different, though. My distorted mind seemed to convince me I had to act. This was my opportunity to end the pain once and for all. I quietly slipped myself under the water and held myself there. It was difficult, but I was determined to do it.

I could hear the *thump, thump, thump* of my heartbeat as my ears sank below the surface. The sound was loud and fast and the only thing

I could hear. I was motionless. There wasn't a splash or even a trickle of water running over the sides of the tub. There was just stillness.

I wanted to die.

I closed my eyes as the air in my lungs had almost run out. The only thought that was running through my head was, "Please God, let me die."

JAY» When I heard Beth slam the bathroom door, I got a terrible feeling in the pit of my stomach. I had seen her act out many times in the past, but something about this particular reaction scared me. I knocked on the door to see if I could come in. She didn't answer. I continued knocking and talking to her from the outside of the very door that would forever change our lives. I assured her that everything would be fine. Still, there was no answer.

I got scared as the seconds ticked into minutes.

I began pushing against the door to see if I could somehow pry it open.

I couldn't budge it.

The door was too thick to kick in, but it was my last resort before having to find an ax to break through or calling the police, which I didn't want to do.

I kicked as hard as I could. The excruciating pain from the impact shot from the heel of my foot to the top of my thigh—but I didn't care. One kick and the door swung wide open. I remember being shocked that the door opened with just one kick. I believe the power of God opened the door.

There before me was the worst possible sight.

Beth was underwater.

She was still.

I had no idea if she was dead or alive.

I rushed toward the tub to grab her and bring her lifeless body to the surface. Her face was pale white. There was no sign of life.

"No!" I screamed as loud as I could.

And then, suddenly, I heard Beth gasp as the air hit her lungs. It was a sound I never want to hear again as long as I live. She was in a daze. I kept yelling and shaking her and then I hugged her and held her for a very long time.

"I love you, Beth. Don't leave me. Don't do this to us." I wept as I gently rocked her.

Beth looked at me with a blank stare. She began to gather herself. She grabbed her robe, bolted out of the bathroom and out the front door. It happened so fast that I barely got to my feet before she was gone.

She ran down the street, barefoot and still soaked from the tub.

Thankfully, one of our neighbors, who happened to be a police officer, saw her as she was running away. The officer flashed the lights from her patrol car at Beth to get her to stop. And, thank God, she did.

When I caught up with Beth, I put my arm around her and began walking home. The officer followed us back into the house, and I explained that Beth was struggling with depression, mentioning nothing of the events that had just taken place for fear that they would take her into the hospital for observation.

That was the worst night of my life.

I remember looking out the window after I had put Beth to bed, feeling like there were demons clawing at the glass. Some dark force wanted my wife that night. I wasn't going to let them get her.

I hid every knife we owned before I went to bed. I made sure to sleep on the top of the bed covers, so if Beth made a move, I would feel it and wake up. Looking back, I don't think I slept a wink that whole night.

The next morning, my brother came to take the kids for a few days so Beth and I could deal with the situation.

We spent the next several days crying, missing the children, and trying to figure things out.

Something had to change.

The problem was that I didn't know how to fix this.

Beth and I talked about redemption and what would have happened if she had succeeded in taking her life that night. That's when we stopped worrying about what anyone else thought and began to get Beth the help she needed to start her long road of healing.

As the days turned into a full week, we both realized this was a wake-up call. Not just for Beth but for both of us.

One thing we were certain of was that stability doesn't come externally—it comes from internal strength. We were committed to maintaining it in our family from that day on.

8 GOD USES ORDINARY PEOPLE TO DO EXTRAORDINARY THINGS

BETH» A few days after my suicide attempt, I came to the realization that I had almost given my kids the same life that I had—a life without a mother. I was broken to the core and could not stop the flood of emotions that this thought brought. God's love and mercy washed over me as I realized that He had rescued me for a second time.

Jay's brother and sister-in-law took our children for a few days while Jay and I began to rebuild our lives. We had let so many little foxes come in and steal parts of our relationship away. We needed to get every thought and emotion out so that we could have a fresh, new beginning. We listened to music, cried, and talked for hours on end. It was the beginning of the healing process, but we knew we still had so far to go.

First up, we wanted to get a second opinion on my medications. I could not function on the drugs they had me on. I knew I had to find another way. A dear friend suggested I see a very wise psychiatrist who was near retirement. Jay and I went to see the doctor together. When I shared my story, his eyes welled up with tears.

"I don't know if it gets any worse than that," he said.

This was the first time I felt heard and understood by a doctor. He took time to listen to me and then shared his thoughts. He did not believe I was bipolar at all. He said I had repressed post-traumatic stress syndrome. He explained that I had experienced extreme trauma as a child, which was the cause for my anxiety, anger, depression, and horrible nightmares. I was no longer able to hold back these intense emotions. I had to come face to face with my past before I could become whole.

I felt such relief. It felt good to have validation from someone with roughly fifty years of experience in the field.

By the time this therapist diagnosed me, I had already been in counseling for a year with little progress. I wanted to wean myself off of the medications but wasn't exactly sure how to break free of the chains I continued to be in. A dear friend recommended I see her counselor for help with the transition.

This particular counselor had five offices around the Twin Cities and had been counseling for approximately twenty-six years. He had been doing traditional counseling for twenty-three when he began an approach that is not as counselor driven as traditional counseling. The counselor is there to facilitate, but God is the one who determines the course. He said he had seen more people set free of their issues in the three years he was using this approach than he had in all of his previous twenty-three years. I was extremely hopeful he would be able to help me.

Jay and I began to see him two times a week for two-hour sessions. I was in counseling for four hours a week, which was intense, but I was thankful beyond belief that we were finally attacking my issues with determination and bulldog tenacity. I knew that continuing to run from my problems through denial or choosing divorce or suicide would only bring more misery and pain. I had to come face to face with my grief, anger, and sadness. I could no longer run.

Throughout the nine months of intense counseling, God revealed areas where I needed deep healing. He showed me seven rooms where the lights were off and the doors were locked. I was afraid to enter these rooms, but one by one God took me by the hand and together we went in and tackled the lies and the pain that resided in each one.

One of the rooms that I could hardly bear to enter was the room that held the pain from my sexual abuse. I often wondered how God could let something like that happen.

Had He abandoned me just like my mother had?

I was taken aback by the intense emotions of anger toward my abusers and toward God.

Where was He while I was being stripped of my innocence?

Did He even care?

As tears streamed out of my eyes, God instantly brought an image into my mind. I was brought back to the exact place of one of the encounters; and I could see myself as a little girl, lying there, feeling helpless. I was alone, or so I thought. This time as I walked back into the memory, I could see Jesus lying there next to me. He was stroking my hair and crying with me.

Why wouldn't He make it stop?

He slowly and gently reminded me of His love and the fact that He has given man a free choice. He did not plan this for my life, but there was evil in the world that man had chosen outside of His perfect will. He expressed His deep love for me and that He was there by my side comforting me through it. He had never left me, not even for a moment. The warmth and comfort of that image has stayed with me ever since. I knew beyond a doubt that He loved me and would never ever leave me.

Another room was the abandonment I felt through my mother's suicide. To be honest, I'm not sure that I ever actually grieved her death as a young girl. I don't remember crying or dealing with the unimaginable loss.

When I would think back to that time period, my emotions were blank—completely gone and lifeless. In the safety of the counselor's office and with Jay by my side, I wept and wailed over the loss of my mother. I remember a deep cleansing sensation coming over me as God began to chip away at the hardened layers of my heart. I was beginning to feel the appropriate emotions that I should have felt long ago. Yet maybe as a five-year-old I wasn't meant to handle them.

My counselor explained that God, in His mercy, has given us a protective mechanism that kicks in when we experience deep pain too young in life. We numb ourselves to survive, but then we unknowingly carry that through life. We never learn to feel because we never go back and deal with the pain in the correct way. Through the release of grieving my mom's death, God was able to reveal to me that my mom was very ill. She loved me and didn't want to walk out of my life. She was hurting, and I saw her in a fresh, new light of compassion; and I was able to forgive her and release the pain. With this epiphany, the sting of abandonment was gone.

I felt His arms wrap around me and heal each of my wounds. I was able to forgive every person in my life that had hurt me and also forgive myself for the myriad of poor choices I had made. One by one, the chains were beginning to fall off as I uncovered the lies I had spent a lifetime believing. I was now beginning to see how much the enemy wanted my destruction. These lies were from him, and he wanted me to be held captive by them. I was not about to let him win. I was beginning to taste freedom and it was sweeter than ever. I wanted more.

God continued to uncover layer after layer in my heart. Issues such as low self-esteem, emotional instability, outbursts of anger, intense shame, an inability to experience true intimacy in marriage, and many others began to be removed from my life.

I was beginning to live with a new identity and freedom. The life of daily trying to keep my head above water that I thought I was destined for was now a thing of the past. I was filled with more joy, peace, and contentment than I had ever known.

Those 144 hours I spent in that counseling office were the most difficult and intense hours of my life. It was hard work, yet the payoff was invaluable. I was able to get off all medication and was finally on the road to full recovery.

God truly transformed my thoughts and beliefs, which was absolutely critical. I had gone through my Christian life believing God's truth in my head; and for the first time, I was able to experience His love and truth in my heart. I realized His promises were for me personally, that He chose to die for me. All of His words became incredibly personal, and I was able to see myself and the world through new eyes.

Toward the end of my counseling, God gave me an image of Him placing a crown on my head and jewels around my neck. He was showing me my royal inheritance in Him. I was no longer filled with shame, believing I was stained, dirty, used goods—I was a child of the King. He then walked me over to a massive oak tree where I could see this beautiful little girl swinging without a care in its branches. That little girl was me, and God was the strong oak tree. I was finally experiencing all the joys of childhood because I was safe in His arms.

God had done a tremendous work on me emotionally, spiritually, and relationally; but the physical element would be the last to come.

About the same time our counseling was coming to completion, Jay was being asked to move our family to Florida to take a job with the headquarters of Great Commission Ministries, the ministry he worked for. We made an investigative trip and after praying, we felt that it was the right thing to do.

In December of 2001, we moved our family to Orlando, Florida. On the road trip there, we found out we were expecting our fourth child. This had been a longing in my heart for years; but since Jay did not share that same desire, I had accepted his decision and proceeded to sell every remnant of baby items we had before we discovered I was pregnant once again. The process of letting go of those items was difficult for me as I truly felt we were supposed to have another boy in our family who was to be named Noah.

It wasn't a regular occurrence for me to get these types of thoughts, and I knew we might be missing out on something. But without Jay being in complete agreement, I knew it wasn't possible, so I surrendered these feelings over to God and was able to let it go.

Once the baby items were sold, the house was packed, and we were on the road, I shared with Jay that I had been feeling nauseated the last few days. He about jumped out of his seat and demanded we stop at the nearest rest stop to take the pregnancy test that I had conveniently brought in my overnight bag. I was just as shocked as he was because we were doing everything possible to prevent this. But as Jay now says, "Natural family planning means plan on a family!" Lo and behold, I was pregnant. Roughly thirty-five weeks later, I gave birth to a nine-pound, ten-ounce baby boy whom we named Noah.

We lived in Orlando for a year and a half while Jay unhappily worked behind a desk doing a job he was not thriving in. We questioned if we'd made the right decision of leaving all of our friends and Jay's family in Minneapolis behind. We knew we didn't want to run back to the safety of familiarity, so we stayed until we knew for sure what we were supposed to do. That year and a half was a desert experience for Jay as he was searching to find out what he was created to do. He was great at sales and had been successful in that, but he now had a deep passion for full-time ministry. He was torn as to what road to take.

I continued to experience freedom in all areas of my life but still knew there was something off in my body. I was constantly battling headaches, fatigue, and stomach pain; and every month when my cycle would hit, I would slump into a mini-depression.

I reached out to a friend of mine who had been working with a Certified Traditional Naturopath—who looks for the root cause of a problem and attempts to educate the client in natural, non-invasive, non heroic ways to address the causes, so that the body can heal itself—and a whole host of health problems were uncovered that needed to be addressed.

The trauma in my life had done a number on my thyroid, adrenals, and hormones. I was completely out of whack and now realized the final piece of the healing puzzle was bringing wholeness to my body. I had failed to recognize that there are four parts to who we are as people—spiritual, emotional, relational, and physical. Trying to address issues by looking at one or two elements is incomplete and unbalanced.

With the guidance, support, and help of my gifted naturopath, I spent the next five years rebuilding my health and correcting the imbalances in my body. She not only served me with her knowledge and skill, but she became a good friend and mentor to me.

Jay now says that he feels like he has gotten a new and improved wife, and I can't tell you how grateful that makes me feel. Of course, I still have my weaknesses and imperfections. I struggle with the usual ups and downs of life. I sometimes snap at my kids, get angry at Jay, and I even have days where I want to stick my kids in school and buy a plot of land out in the middle of nowhere! What I do notice, though, is that what I feel is normal, and that feels good.

» » » » »

We know that God uses broken people to spread His message. At the end of the day, no one is perfect. We sure aren't. We all have issues. We're human beings, which means we will have flaws. Some of us use those experiences that created hurt and disappointment in our lives as a crutch, while others may choose to use them as a reason to do more, be better, and create a new pattern so they can share their journey with the idea of helping others who may be going through or have already been through similar situations.

After giving it a lot of thought, we both agreed that sharing Beth's story was important and would inevitably become a big part of our future. We understand the power of God and His ability to use even the darkest situations for good. We had no way of knowing that Beth's life experiences would someday impact others by showing them that you can overcome anything with a relationship with Jesus.

CHALLENGE #4
God Uses Ordinary People to Do Extraordinary Things

»» »» »» »» »» »» »» »» »» »» »» »» »» »» »» »» »» »» »» »»

Everything is opposite with God. He loves to use the weak and broken things in the world to astound the wise. You may think your life is a complete mess, and you wonder how anything good can come from your past. The truth is that God is able to take the broken pieces of your life and build a beautiful mosaic that displays His love and grace. The Bible says that His power is perfected in weakness. He's in the business of changing and redeeming lives. One of our favorite passages in the Bible is Acts 4:13, in which Peter and John stand before the rulers of Jerusalem with great courage. Upon seeing the courage they had, they realized that they were average, ordinary men who had been with Jesus. Just being with Him makes all the difference in the world no matter how ordinary you think you are.

Mark Horvath went from riches to rags. He worked in Hollywood where he had a successful career in television syndication, drove a Mercedes Benz, and had a coveted reserved parking spot at work. After years of illicit drug use and a string of bad choices, he found himself on the Hollywood streets, homeless. He felt abandoned and hopeless. Things got so bad that he even contemplated taking his own life. His life turned around after giving himself to God, attending Alcoholics Anonymous, and getting involved with a church in Los Angeles called the Dream Center. Through the Dream Center he realized that the pain, despair, and brokenness he experienced while living on the streets could be leveraged to help others in the same position he was in. He is now a leading voice and advocate for the homeless as well as the founder of an organization called Invisible People. Mark now interviews homeless people and shares their unedited stories on his website: www.invisiblepeople.tv. God is using Mark, an ordinary person, to do extraordinary things.

Your life may be far different from Mark's. But still, you may feel ordinary, possibly even insignificant. Your past might seem like a heavy weight that you carry with you wherever you go. Your weakness is actually your greatest strength. The apostle Paul wrote in 2 Corinthians 11:30, "If I must boast, I will boast of the things that show my weakness." In the next chapter, 2 Corinthians 12:9, he wrote, "But he said to me, 'My grace is sufficient for you, for my power is made perfect in weakness.'" It's in seeing the full extent of our weakness that we understand God's power. He can take your past and redeem it for the present.

> » Will you allow God to take all the broken pieces of your past and allow Him to create something beautiful with your life?
> » What is the weakness you carry with you, and what strength, what clarity of focus, can you find within it?

We challenge you to give Him your life and see what He can create. He has the ability to take the ordinary and make it extraordinary.

9 EVERYONE MATTERS

OCTOBER 2007

JAY» Most people go through life looking at people and judging them by their appearance. It's so easy to attach a label and only see that person as homeless or rich, thin or fat, black or white. The reality is that we all play different roles in the world. We were all created in God's image; therefore, we all have dignity, regardless of who we are or what our supposed standing in society is.

Shortly before we left for our mission trip to Africa, I attended a three-day spiritual retreat in the North Georgia mountains. It was there that I met an unforgettable man named Seven. He was rough, drove a Harley Davidson, had a long, white Fu Manchu moustache and looked tough—very tough.

When we first met, Seven shared that he had spent several years in the mafia where he worked as an enforcer. He eventually spent seven years in prison too—much of that time in solitary confinement—for his involvement with organized crime. Although he wasn't allowed to have many items in his jail cell, the prison officials did oblige his request for a Bible—an odd request since Seven was illiterate. He had never read a single word in his life. Miraculously, he was somehow able to read the Bible! To this day, the Bible is still the only book he can actually read.

During his incarceration, Seven developed his own private

relationship with God. When he was finally let out of prison, he knew exactly what he was supposed to do. He wanted to spend time under the freeway bridges of Atlanta and rescue the hurting and homeless.

"Son, you're going to come under the bridges with me someday," Seven said, staring me down as if I were his next target.

Until he explained the situation, I had absolutely no clue that just twenty minutes from our home there is a large population of homeless people who live under the freeway bridges. The mere concept had never even crossed my mind.

"Yeah, sure, I'll go with you, Seven," I said, probably more out of fear than desire.

Strangely, there was something I found exciting and intriguing about the idea. When we began asking other people if they had ever heard about these makeshift communities, some said they had, but most said they had not. I didn't give much thought to it after that because my spare time was being spent preparing for our mission trip.

However, shortly after we came back from Africa, Seven and the thought of going under the bridges started creeping into my thoughts. Several people from our trip talked about wanting to go back to Africa to serve, but I couldn't forget the images Seven had planted in my mind about all of the people in my own backyard that needed help too.

For obvious reasons, I suddenly wanted to check out what Seven was doing. I wanted to see with my own eyes what I had unknowingly been overlooking all of these years.

After discussing it, Beth and I decided it would be good to bring the whole family on our first visit under the bridges. We had become such a tight family unit that we wanted to experience it together.

Deciding to bring the kids with us wasn't an easy decision to make because we really had no idea what the experience would be like. It was definitely out of our comfort zone. Neither of us was sure it was completely safe or appropriate for them, especially Bekah, Abigail, and Noah.

Even though we'd be going with other people who had been under the bridges before, we still were unsure if bringing the kids was the right thing to do. I thought it was interesting that none of the folks we were going with had ever brought their children under the bridges because they worried about exposing them to the scene down there. In a strange way, that was one of my strongest arguments to bring our kids. I wanted them to see and experience how some people live differently than we do. Plus, if I thought I was putting my family in danger in any way, I believed Seven would have stopped me. I completely trusted him.

Seven agreed to meet us there. We told the children we didn't know what to expect, but we should go into the experience with no judgments, open hearts, and lots of love. Since all of us (except Noah) had just been to Africa, this advice was easy for them to grasp. I think they were more excited at the prospect of helping others than we were. They genuinely wanted to go.

We all arrived in our minivan, while Seven came rolling up on his Harley Davidson motorcycle. The children were very taken with Seven from the second he arrived. He was very kind and gentle with them, even giving Abigail and Noah a ride on the back of his Harley.

I have to admit that being under the bridges was uncomfortable at first. It smelled awful. The scent of urine was so overpowering, it was actually hard to breathe. The cement was slippery in places from people defecating too. There were a few moments I worried one of us might actually slip and fall. If that happened, we could drop around ten feet into the sharp slanted cement underpass beneath the bridge.

As we toured this underground community, we prayed with many of the people we met, gave them the food we brought with us, and offered our support by simply lending a kind listening ear. For the most part, the people under the bridges were very welcoming, extremely memorable, and some even took us by surprise.

For example, we met a man whose appearance reminded Beth of her brother Jimmy, who had taken his life several years earlier. He had bright eyes and a warm smile. When we spoke, he looked right at us and said, "I see love in your eyes. I can tell you guys are for real."

This man shared that he had come from a well-to-do family but had made several bad decisions over the years that landed him in this unexpected place—divorced, out of touch with his children, living under a bridge, and addicted to alcohol. We felt his burden and tried to convince him that he didn't have to live that way. He hung on our words and seemed to want out of this lifestyle, but the fear of the unknown held him captive.

We met another man who was so well dressed, it was hard to comprehend that he too called this bridge community home. He wore a stark, crisp, clean white shirt and tailored pants. He showed us his area where he lived, which he kept immaculate. He wasn't a drunk, derelict, or crazy person. He was clean, sober, and clear. When we asked him why he was living under the bridges instead of a shelter, he showed us his prideful side.

"I got myself here. I'll get myself out," he said.

One of the most unforgettable guys we met looked like a character straight out of *Pirates of the Caribbean*. He had a long scraggly beard and slurred his words from drinking a little too much beer. We spent time talking to this man. The old man listened as we spoke. He was taking us in as much as we were taking him in.

"Show me what you say," he said.

I wasn't really sure what he said at first, so I asked him to repeat himself.

"Show me what you say!" he slowly said, only this time with more emphasis and enunciation than the first time.

I wondered how many people had said things to this man and had never followed through. It reminded me of a verse in the Bible, James 2:17, that says, "Faith without works is dead." Faith is demonstrated by acting and living out what you believe. That's where the rubber hits the road. It's not about what we say—it's about what we do.

Evidently, he was calling us out. He was telling us to put our money where our mouth was.

I've never forgotten those insightful words because that was the moment I believe we realized that so many people talk about doing things and never act on it. The old homeless man was calling us to action. That encounter confirmed our desire to act and do something about our faith. It also inspired us to never give up on our mission to serve.

When I saw my then five-year-old son Noah hugging homeless guys with no fear, trepidation, or judgment, we all realized how extremely powerful this experience was and what a privilege it was to share it together as a family.

» » » » »

That special day left the most profound impression on all of us. Even the hardest guys living under the bridges had tears in their eyes with the love they received from our children. It touched their hearts to see a family bring their children into that environment. The fact that we included our kids in the experience sent a very loving message— one we didn't necessarily plan but are glad we made. As a result, the people warmed up to us right away.

We never came across anyone who was harmful or inappropriate. Some of the guys looked a little scary at first, but once you see past their exterior and look into their eyes, you can see into their souls. These were good people who had fallen on hard times. They were someone's child, husband, wife, father, brother, mother, or sister. However you describe them, this was the start of seeing people for who they really are and in the way God sees them—the whole them.

We had all the confirmation we needed after that experience. There was no doubt that traveling the country serving others was what we were being called to do. There was a tremendous amount of peace in knowing that we were answering that call.

By the end of October, we were committed to the RV and were starting to plan for our journey. We immediately put our house up for sale and waited for the perfect buyer to come along.

In the meantime, we began to unload everything of value that we wouldn't be able to take with us. We spent the next six months letting go of and releasing our attachment to unnecessary things. To say this purging was a process would be underselling just how hard that experience was on everyone.

On one hand, it was cleansing and cathartic. We had spent years acquiring stuff that now seemed meaningless. On the other hand, deciding what to bring and what to leave behind was no easy task—especially for our children, who were used to having so much.

We all understood the limitations we faced swapping our spacious forty-five-hundred square feet of living space for the three hundred or so feet we'd all be sharing in the RV. It wasn't easy telling our kids, "No, you cannot bring that favorite stuffed animal or extra remote-controlled car," but we all had to make sacrifices, and limiting our possessions was one of them.

We sold as much of our old things as we could bear, gave lots of it away, and arranged for two storage units in Atlanta to store the rest we couldn't quite give up, including most of the brand-new furniture we had just bought to finish decorating our home. When we decided to make this trip, we had just finished up three years of perfecting and redecorating. We pondered the idea of selling it all, but we also didn't want to find ourselves six months down the road having to repurchase everything again if things didn't work out.

And even though we had to adjust our thinking as we began to disassemble the only life we had all known, God continued to confirm that we were doing the right thing.

One of the most memorable transactions was selling our almost-new Honda Odyssey minivan. The vehicle was less than a year old when we decided it didn't make sense to keep it for our trip. We placed an ad in the local papers, asking a fair price for the car and its condition.

We received a call from a gentleman who said he was very interested in the van but wasn't able to afford our asking price. He and his wife came to see the car anyway, hoping we might be willing to negotiate. They wanted to buy it but made a low-ball offer that we had to turn down. To be candid, we weren't sure if he was tactfully negotiating or trying to work us over.

Something kept tugging at us, though, telling us he was for real. To be certain, the extra few dollars would have helped us, but we instinctively knew the difference would have a much bigger effect on their lives than our own.

We waited a couple of hours, hoping we'd hear back from the couple, but no phone call ever came. Still, we couldn't shake this feeling that we were supposed to sell them our car.

We decided to call them and offer the car for a fair compromise between their offer and our bottom line price. When we phoned them back, for whatever reason, we said we would let the vehicle go for less. We didn't plan on giving up the extra few hundred dollars. It just happened.

The car was an absolute steal at the price he bought it at, yet something assured us we were doing the right thing. The couple said they wanted the car but felt they should come see it one more time before agreeing to the deal.

JAY» When Baskar and his wife arrived, I asked if they believed in God. They said they did and that they were Christians. I shared with them that I felt God had told us to bless them, so that was why we came down in price. We shook hands and made the deal.

The following day, I couldn't help but feel like I had given the car away. I received an e-mail from another prospective buyer who was interested at a much higher price. I began to question whether I had made the right decision in selling it to Baskar. I even contemplated backing out so that I could get more money, knowing we had many moving expenses coming up. This is exactly the type of transaction that always gave me an internal struggle because I was all about making the most money I could. As I wrestled through all this in my mind, I received an e-mail from the man I had shaken hands with and sold the vehicle to.

Dear Jay,

*I am out of words. All I know is that this came in spite of me...
and it feels very good even now to know that you and Beth felt
God's will in making this decision. Actually, I have a confession
to make. My wife and I had decided yesterday morning about
the maximum we could stretch our offer to. We prayed about
it and decided that it would not be God's will for us if you felt
the lowest offer that would make sense to you was above that
amount. And as I told you before, I didn't want to negotiate and
go back and forth to try and lower the price.*

*After you printed out the Blue Book values and did the
math, you told us the lowest you would go. I felt a little sadness,
but I also felt free. The last thing I wanted was to force you to
settle for something below what you could get. So we left. That's
why when you called later in the day and then when I told my
wife that your offer was exactly what we could afford, we were
both speechless. We knew beyond question that God was at
work! It was literally as if we had told God what we could pay,
and He had told you and Beth!*

I wept when I read his letter. I was able to release the doubt I had
because I could feel God saying He wanted to bless that family and
couldn't if I held to my price. Because of the blessing they received, it
turns out that the buyers were able to sell their car to someone they
knew from work for less than they wanted for it, paying the blessing
forward in a way I could never have anticipated.

After that, I realized that God didn't bless me with good fortune so I
could hoard it for myself. He blessed me so I could bless others in return.

When they came to our house to pick up their new car, we all took
a photo together standing in our front room as if we were old friends.
There were so many moments like this that gave us the courage and determination to stay on our path. Somehow, we had gotten so caught up in
money and our things that we had forgotten how important relationships

are. That transaction helped us to realize that people matter more than our things.

After we came back from Africa, I no longer wanted to work in an office environment. I didn't feel connected to that lifestyle anymore, but I still needed to make a living. Since I was a mortgage broker, I figured I could pretty much set up shop wherever I wanted. The bulk of my business was being done over the phone and the Internet, so an office wasn't crucial to my success. That's when I began working out of our home.

Everything seemed to be going well for the first few months—that is, until the market began to crumble. I went from getting several mortgages a day to begging for my loans to get approved.

My parents were at their house in Tucson for the winter and suggested we come out for a few weeks to visit. Since our house was on the market, we welcomed the opportunity to get away. When you are selling a home, you have to be ready on a moment's notice to show the house. We were constantly cleaning and tidying our home to make sure it was ready to be seen. We were all too happy to leave the house in perfect condition for a month or so, hoping someone would come along and buy it while we were gone.

We decided to go to Arizona for the month of December. We stayed in a small two-bedroom house my father owned next door to their place for the next five weeks.

Being in Tucson gave us the opportunity to experience what life on the road might be like. We got a sense of living in a smaller space, what working on the road would be like, and how being away from Atlanta would impact us. It was a small taste of the road ahead.

I got up very early to get my work done so I could spend the rest of the day with my family. I began work at 6:00 a.m. so I could make my calls to clients on the East Coast every morning. I had my laptop, and I spent the bulk of those five weeks working so I knew for sure I'd be able to do my job from the RV while we were on the road. None of my clients knew I was thousands of miles away from Atlanta or in a different time zone. I was able to offer my clients the same service without missing a beat. This made it clear that my physical location didn't matter—only my accessibility, which was easy with modern technology.

The ease in which I made the transition was inspiring. I actually believed I could keep on working as if nothing had changed. I was closing deals without getting up, putting on a suit, and trudging through corporate America.

We came back from Arizona fired up and ready to take the next step. Unfortunately, we had to wait months for the right buyer for our home to come along.

So many people looked at it with great enthusiasm. "Oh, we love it!" they'd say; and then we never heard from them again.

We hoped we would sell the house by December as we could see what was happening in the real estate market overall. Prices were tumbling, and fast. When we first had the house appraised in October, the price came in at $425,000. By January, only three months later, it had dropped to $400,000.

We could feel the pressure mounting with every passing month it stood on the market. If we couldn't sell the house, there was no possible way for us to pursue our dream. We'd have to stay put and find a plan B.

By this time, we had all given in to the adventure that was ahead of us. Selling the house was the determining factor between dream and reality. It had gotten to the point where we didn't care if we had to take less money than we wanted as long as it sold for a fair price. We'd compensate by buying a less decked-out RV.

The more we waited for a buyer, the more we wanted to leave. We were done with that house. If we had any doubts left, they waned with time. We wanted out. Beth no longer wanted to clean all the time, and I was sick of taking care of everything and all of the responsibility. We both had gotten to a place where we despised having to garden, mow the lawn, and pick up fallen leaves. Our hearts had definitely changed. We were ready for a change of scenery. It's like deciding to leave your job. Once you've made the decision, it is kind of hard to stick around when your heart is somewhere else.

And then, one day we thought our prayers had been answered when a couple made an offer. We were so excited until we heard they were backing out to purchase another home they liked better than ours…and for more money! That was a real disappointment to us.

Finally, in April 2008, six months after we initially listed the property, we handed the keys over to a couple who came to see our house and knew they had found their new home. When they walked through the house the first day they came to see it, they said they felt a presence—a warmth that led them to make an offer. Although they didn't have kids, they knew this was the house where they'd someday raise their family together. They said meeting our family and sensing the joy we shared in that home was all they needed to know they were making the right decision. We were completely blown away by them and knew they were the family we had been waiting for.

》 》 》 》 》

Once we knew the house was officially sold, we could begin pursuing our dream and search for our new home on wheels. Before we listed the house on the market, we took a home-equity line of credit to get the extra money we would need to buy the RV. We would use this money to purchase an RV while we waited to close on the house. We had spent the time waiting doing lots of research on what we wanted in an RV. There are so many different layouts to choose from. We had to figure out what the needs of our family were so we could narrow down the choices. We knew that we'd need an extra room that could serve as an office for me since I would still be selling mortgages and would need a place to work. A friend who owned an RV suggested we consider a diesel pusher motor home.

Diesel pushers are the largest and most luxurious when it comes to RVs. The engine is located in the rear of the vehicle, hence the name *pusher*. By the time we narrowed down all of our needs, we decided on a forty-foot Monaco Knight. We found three on the Internet that were available in our price range. All of them were located somewhere west of the Rockies. We spoke to an owner in late March who lived in Las Vegas. He told us that he and his wife wanted to unload their RV because she had taken ill and they were moving out of the country. They were planning a trip to Tennessee in a few weeks and offered to drive the RV out to us, at no obligation or extra cost. We were very appreciative of their offer, but we didn't feel right about it, since at the time, we still hadn't officially closed on the house. If the buyer fell through, we wouldn't have the money to purchase the RV. Since we were willing to pay for plane tickets to look at the three vehicles we had found, we decided to put that money toward the cost of gas for this man's trip. We agreed and made sure he understood there would be no further obligation if we didn't like what we saw.

We were expecting the prospective RV at our home a few weeks after we first talked. Even though we had been shopping for an RV for a few months, we were completely mesmerized by the forty-foot machine that drove through our neighborhood and landed in front of our house. We knew what to expect, yet it was the craziest sight. We calculated that we'd be hauling a total length of sixty-five feet once we added our motorcycle and the Honda Pilot we planned to tow in the back along with our six bicycles. To say it was a bit daunting would be the understatement of the year!

We all jumped aboard to check out our potential new home. The kids kept saying how cool they thought it was while we walked through the little more than 340 square feet of living space wondering if we could really make this work. Our enthusiasm couldn't be dampened. The RV even had a washer and dryer, something we didn't expect but thought was a terrific bonus.

Much to our surprise, it actually felt larger than we anticipated. The office in the back was exactly what we needed. The RV had beautiful wood cabinetry, which made it feel homey. There was plenty of storage space inside and underneath the vehicle, which would become essential down the road.

And finally, the extra push was that the price was right. It was less than the other two RVs we found, and it was already at our door. It seemed as if God had given us a gift and even delivered it right to us. We said we'd take it on the spot. Even with the money we had in our equity line, we were still around ten thousand dollars short. Thankfully, Jay's dad lent us the money, and we agreed to pay him back from money we received when we closed on the house.

The transaction happened so fast! In fact, looking back, despite our eagerness, at the time it felt kind of suspicious. We couldn't help but wonder if their story wasn't the whole truth.

Were they unloading a lemon?

Was there something wrong with the RV?

We were about to give these people all of the money we had and then some, without having the vehicle thoroughly checked out and inspected. If we were buying into major problems, we wouldn't have enough extra cash to keep ourselves afloat. We hoped and prayed the couple wasn't conning us as we drove them to the bank to pick up a rather substantial cashier's check that was ready to go.

As an added twist, the wife suddenly fainted at the bank. We weren't sure what to think of the episode. Was it a stunt or was she truly ill? As much as we wanted to show her compassion, we had no way of knowing the truth. We were very nervous that something wasn't right but chose to proceed anyway.

The man we bought the RV from had to get some paperwork done for transferring the extended warranty over to us, so we were able to hold back a small portion of the final payment until that was complete. It wasn't much, but it felt like a safety net if things somehow went south.

After the couple left, our entire family climbed into the RV. Jay sat behind the wheel with no idea how to drive the thing!

We were dying to go for a ride but didn't have the foggiest idea how to turn on the ignition.

Uh-oh.

What had we done?

We were the proud owners of a forty-foot vehicle we couldn't budge from the driveway of a house we were just days away from no longer owning.

We decided to call the former owner to ask him for some tips. He had left us less than an hour earlier.

"You're scaring me," he said. "You need to take a class on how to use everything before you hit the road."

We were able to assure him that if he could walk us through the ignition process, we'd be able to handle the rest from there. Thank goodness he was a patient man. Of course, he also had almost $140,000 of ours in his pocket too—that may have inspired him to want to help us.

We drove our new home to Chick-fil-A, a favorite restaurant of ours, for dinner. It was so much fun. The kids were beside themselves, basking in the new adventures that were ahead for all of us. We spent the next two weeks in the RV, familiarizing ourselves with every bell and whistle as we packed it up before finally hitting the road.

Now, we have both managed many projects over the years, but coordinating a move from our house to our new home was no easy task. It was like doing a life-sized jigsaw puzzle, trying to figure out what we could fit and where it should go. When the vehicle is full, we are carrying approximately thirty-three thousand pounds. That's sixteen and a half tons!

Some RVs have shallow compartments underneath, but the one we bought had four separate deep storage areas on the bottom. We had the good fortune of having more storage space than expected—and boy, did we need it! We packed all of our necessities along with tennis rackets, roller blades, golf clubs, and lots of other goodies to use on our great adventure.

We were able to figure out a logical way to place our seasonal clothes in bins and store them in the back when we weren't in need of heavy sweaters, snow boots, and winter jackets. Storage bins and labels became our two best friends for the next couple of weeks.

As our departure date neared, we wanted to tie up all of our financial loose ends. We took the money we had left over from the sale of our house and paid everything off in full. We wanted to embark on this new chapter of our lives completely debt free. Except for our day-to-day expenses, we had zero debt. That was an amazing feeling.

And though there wasn't a large amount of money left over after we paid every last bill, we did have a small nest egg, just in case something unexpected came up. We managed to pack up the house and RV with only days to spare before our departure, but not without a lot of stress and exhaustion. During those days we also exercised lots of faith and prayer to strengthen us for the journey ahead.

On the night before we left to start our exciting new life, our closest friends from Atlanta threw us a going-away party. We drove the RV to the party because we had to be completely out of the house that same day.

By that time, almost everyone had finally accepted that we were actually going through with our crazy dream. And anyone who still had their doubts became believers the night of the party as we proudly gave tours of our new home.

People gave us journals to keep track of every moment, gift cards to use on the road, and above all, showered us with love and support. The funniest gift we received was the DVD of the movie *RV*. (This would later become one of the most common questions we are asked—"Have you seen the movie *RV*?" The answer is YES, more times than we care to admit!) Seeing everyone together for one last time really drove home the reality of what we were about to embark upon.

We watched as our two daughters cried, huddled together with their best girlfriends, while several of Ben's buddies decided to wrap the RV in plastic wrap, which we thought was hysterically funny. There were lots of hugs and tears going around most of the night for all of us.

Saying good-bye to our friends was bittersweet. On one hand, it was a final farewell to our old way of life. But the door to our dream had finally been swung fully open, and it was time to take that next giant step through it and start moving toward our goal.

God plants a unique dream and passion in each of us. For us, it happened to include selling our house, buying an RV, and traveling with purpose. We came alive when we started to pursue our dream. And even though the many and winding roads that led us here weren't easy, we felt an incredible sense of freedom and excitement about the possibility and potential of whatever was ahead for us.

 CHALLENGE #5
Everyone Matters

»»»

We live in a society that is consumed with how we look. As a country, we spend billions of dollars on beauty products, weight loss systems, and cosmetic surgery. We are obsessed with our outward appearance without taking the time to nurture our inner selves. If it makes you feel any better, this is something that people have struggled with since biblical times. When it was time for Samuel to anoint a new king in Israel, God was clear that Samuel was not to consider the new king's appearance. He said to Samuel, "'The LORD does not look at the things man looks at. Man looks at the outward appearance, but the LORD looks at the heart'" (I Samuel 16:7).

Because we focus on the external, we tend to group ourselves with others of similar backgrounds, life circumstances, and socio-economic statuses. It becomes easy to label people, especially those who are far different from us. We refer to people as homeless, addicts, prostitutes, pedophiles, or a variety of other titles. In reality, we all have more than just one role in life. Someone who's homeless isn't just homeless. They are someone's son or daughter. They might be a husband or wife, father or mother, or they may even be a musician, an artist, or an athlete. When we look at people only as we see them on the outside, we miss who they are as a whole person.

If someone doesn't look, dress, or make as much money as us, our tendency is to judge them, causing an us-versus-them mentality. Whether we admit it or not, this is something that most of us struggle with. In fact, social research reveals that the average person thinks they are better than the average person.

Thankfully God doesn't judge us on our outward appearance. When He looks at us, He looks at our hearts. He views us from the inside out. Regardless of what we look like or our socio-economic status, we are all made in God's image; and we are worthy of dignity and respect. Genesis 1:27 says, "So God created man in his own image, in the image of God he created him; male and female he created them."

Since everyone matters to God, everyone should matter to us, regardless of their appearance or the perceived role that they play in society. Everyone is worthy of dignity and respect because we are all made in the image of God.

» Which people in your life do you sometimes, if not always, ignore?
» Will you begin to view people the way God sees them and get to know them for who they really are inside?

We challenge you to go out of your way and extend your hand to someone who looks far different from you. Take the time to get to know them from the inside out. You might find that you are the one who is changed in the process.

10 THE ARK TOUR

APRIL 19, 2008

We decided our trip should have a name. After several family discussions we settled on calling our journey the ARK Tour. We chose ARK because it was an acronym for Acts of Random Kindness. After all, that was exactly why we were heading out on the road in the first place. We figured the RV would serve as our personal ark, complete with our very own Noah!

We planned on leaving Atlanta midmorning for our first stop— Panama City, Florida. Despite our best efforts to leave on time, we didn't pull out until around noon that day. Since things had been so hectic and chaotic between selling the house, moving, and downsizing to an RV, we hadn't taken a spring break vacation with the kids yet. In fact, we kept the kids schooled all throughout that time because we knew we'd eventually have some downtime when we finally hit the road, and we knew we'd need a break once everything was said and done.

The transition was stressful and hard on all of us. We were all in great need of some rest and relaxation so we could chill out, recharge our batteries, and be totally on our A game. That is why we decided to make the beach our first destination.

Jay drove the entire time, while Beth spent time with Noah, reading books and playing games. Our other children were on the computer or reading. It was a terrifically fun way to travel. Ten hours after pulling out of Atlanta, we arrived at our very first RV resort. We cautiously parked the RV (something we were still perfecting), got settled in, and hit the hay in our new home.

It was nothing short of amazing.

There was a certain serenity we both shared lying in bed together that night. We had every single thing that was important to us in the world contained within the walls and belly of the RV. We could get up at a moment's notice, unplug, and go anywhere, any time. The very thought of that kind of freedom was exhilarating. It was exactly what we imagined when we fantasized about living this way.

We spent the next several days soaking up the sun and experiencing the adventure of the unknown. It was spectacular spending so much time outdoors. We played in the ocean, laughed, splashed, and buried each other in the sand. It was fun to walk on the beach with no obligations, appointments, and nowhere else to be and simply watch the sunset at the end of every day.

We spent those first days without a care in the world, making our biggest task digging and catching sand crabs with the kids. Ben was smart enough to think of bringing salad tongs and a bag for his catches. All in all, we got seven sand crabs and brought them home to cook up for dinner. Unfortunately, all of the meat from the crabs we caught added up to about a tablespoon of meat. It turned out that these types of crabs weren't meant to be eaten.

These were definite moments to treasure. Even something as mundane as finding the nearest grocery store became fun and exciting.

Watching television in the RV on the tiny twenty-four-inch flat screen was different from the comfort of our old living room that had a gigantic fifty-inch plasma TV; yet it was every bit as fun, if not more intimate, than it used to be.

We celebrated Beth's thirty-ninth birthday on April 24, spending time at the beach. That night, we ate dinner together at a restaurant that was located directly on the beach. The host said she was giving us the "best seat in the house," a corner booth on the upper outdoor deck overlooking the ocean.

We watched the most magical sunset that only God could create. It was cloudy when we got to the restaurant, but suddenly, the skies opened and the sun came shining through on the horizon. This sunset was so special and one we would not soon forget.

The way we kicked off our trip felt awesome. We had become like so many American families back in Atlanta—close but not bonded. We shared our lives but hadn't "done" life together. Spending time at the beach, swimming, riding our bikes, and laughing every single day for that first week really brought home what we had been missing in our family.

Another point was driven home those first few days too. Sitting on the beach watching the sunsets and the tide roll in and out was a beautiful reminder that God is all around us. It wasn't hard to appreciate His presence as we watched the sun set into the horizon of the blue-green ocean. The pink, orange, and purple hues illuminated the twilight sky like strokes from a giant paintbrush that could only be held by the hand of God. It wasn't until we went to Topsail Hill Preserve State Park, one of the most beautiful beaches we have ever seen, that it struck us, maybe for the first time, that moments like *this* were why we left Atlanta.

Not long after that sunset at Topsail, we began to dissect the true meaning and purpose of our new life on the road. We both wanted to define our passion and purpose. As we talked, we kept going back to the simple idea of serving those in need.

With every passing day, we found ourselves getting into deeper conversations with each other about our life, plans, expectations, hopes, dreams, and goals for this journey and also for each of our lives. We enjoyed these talks every bit as much as the quiet time we each took by ourselves in the morning to reflect, think, and pray.

What were *His* plans for us?

What did *He* want us to do?

How could we best serve *God* through our journey?

Our purpose was unpretentious—to live simply, to love our family, and to serve others. Now all we had to do was figure out how we would make this new life of service happen.

We had been on the road for a week, and we were still getting used to the whole experience of living in the RV. We were quickly learning and refining how long it took to set up and break down each time we made a stop someplace. Even a small move to just a few miles down the road was a big deal, especially in the beginning. Even though it was stressful at times, the uncertainty was also very exciting too. We were really never sure of what to expect, what would happen next, where we were headed, where we would stay, and whom we would meet.

We've never really been big planners; we are more "wingers," so the adjustment to this transient lifestyle wasn't a hard one to adapt to for us. We rather enjoyed the "where should we go next" conversations that always came with the option of changing our minds at the last minute. We were totally okay with the unknown and spontaneous nature of our adventure. After all, that's what we wanted. As the old saying goes, "Be careful what you wish for. You just might get it!"

11 BLACK WATER

There's one question we get about living in the RV that people seem to be extremely curious about. People we meet want to know how we deal with "black water." Now, for those of you that don't know what black water is, it is not a political cover-up or some type of covert mission. It's the yucky stuff that collects in a holding tank that has to go somewhere.

Okay—here are some basics.

All self-contained RVs have black- and gray-water systems. The toilet runs to the black-water tank while all of the other water we use, from showers to dishes, runs to the gray. Most campsites have sewer hook-ups so you can dump both tanks whenever you need to. Of course, no one ever goes over the task at hand before buying the vehicle. After you own one is also not a great time to try to figure out this process.

JAY» On the first day of our trip, we stopped at a really down-and-dirty campground so we could get the hang of things. I did my best to empty the black water, but I made more of a mess than anything else. Ben videotaped the entire escapade, which everyone thought was really funny—except maybe me. I ended up with gunk all over myself. Luckily, a good friend connected me with his brother-in-law, who spent a lot of time RVing and lived near Panama City—our first stop. He came by to give us a three-hour tutorial. He gave me a general overview of how to care for an RV, which included showing me what valves to open and close, how to attach the hoses, and the best way to handle the process of dumping the water-filled tanks. We can usually go about two to three days on gray water if we take short, military showers and about five days or so before having to dump the black water.

You can only dump your water at designated sewers that can be found at some roadside rest stops and campgrounds. Sometimes it can be really hard to find a dumping site, which has made for a few memorable experiences on the road.

We once parked in my brother Bryan's driveway for two weeks when we were visiting family in Minnesota. I would go out on stealth missions after dark to dump my gray water tanks on his yard. It was an especially dry summer that year, so his entire lawn was brown and scorched from the sun, everywhere, that is, except for where we dumped our gray water. That section of his yard was lush and green. Had I known that gray water was such a good fertilizer I would have been more careful to spread out the love.

After about a week in my brother's driveway, I thought I had gotten away with a desperate dump in what I thought was a local sewer on his street. With no other options, I decided to inconspicuously pull our forty-foot RV in the middle of broad daylight over the manhole cover and make a go at dumping our waste. Shortly after I started dumping, flashing red and blue lights were slowly creeping toward me. Someone had called the police and told them there was a suspicious vehicle in the neighborhood. As the officer approached me I frantically closed the black water valve and opened the gray water valve. He looked me straight in the eye and asked me if I was dumping my black water. I sheepishly looked back at him knowing that I was busted. I was tempted to lie, but I came clean and admitted that I was guilty as charged. I told him that I thought it was okay to dump my waste in the manhole cover because it said sewer. He then explained that what I was dumping my waste into was actually only for rainwater and it went directly into the streams. That was one of the most embarrassing moments of my entire life! I anticipated that he would read me my Miranda rights and slap on some cuffs, but thankfully he showed me mercy. I wanted to dig a hole in my brother's yard and crawl into it when a city worker came and opened up the fire hydrant, allowing the water to clean the sewer where I had deposited our waste. I never did tell my brother about the whole ordeal—I guess he knows now.

It's a dirty job, and thankfully, we've gotten much better at the process. It's been a part of the tradeoff we've learned to live with as part of our new life on the road.

12 THE KINDNESS OF STRANGERS

MAY 3, 2008
NEW ORLEANS, LOUISIANA

We left Florida to make our way northwest. We were headed to Kansas City, where we needed to be by May 6, because Beth's niece was getting married, and we wanted to attend the wedding. We didn't like having any commitments at this point, but knowing we had to be in the middle of the country gave us the opportunity to map out our intended destinations without foolishly zigzagging our way. Gas prices were soaring so we had to be smart in our decisions on where to go and how to get there.

We all agreed to make one of our first stops New Orleans. We were interested in visiting this city that was hit so hard by Hurricane Katrina back in 2005.

As we pulled into downtown New Orleans, we were astonished at the devastation that still existed. We wanted to stop but couldn't find a safe place to park the RV. I was still pretty green with knowing where we could and couldn't drive. Some roads are too narrow while others prohibit vehicles such as ours. It was all still fairly new and it took some time for me to get comfortable with making the right decisions. Remember, we were pulling approximately sixty-five feet of product down the road, which takes a lot of getting used to.

As we pulled into the city limits, I made a turn onto a residential street. I realized after I made the turn that the RV was too tall to clear the trees that lined the road. We could hear branches cracking as they scratched away at the roof of the RV.

I began freaking out, not knowing how much damage the trees were doing to the top of the RV. I tried to find the quickest exit out of this neighborhood, except the turn was too sharp for me to make. I didn't have enough room to clear the corner with all of our cargo in the back. I had to get out and release the car from the tow hitch, back it up, and park it before I could budge the RV.

A lineup of cars had gathered behind us. They were not amused by my inexperience. To make matters worse, there was a car directly in my path. If I moved the RV in either direction, I would have sideswiped that vehicle. I went for help to one of the neighbors who had now gathered in their yards watching in disbelief that someone would be stupid enough to pull an RV the size of ours onto their street.

"Does anyone know who owns this car?" I politely asked, hoping someone would have an answer.

"Yeah," a stranger said. "The owner lives in the apartment over there." He pointed toward a building to my left. Luckily, the guy was home and was able to move his car before I inadvertently moved it for him. The cars that were now stuck behind our vehicles were really ticked at me. As we drove out of the neighborhood, we saw a street sign that read, "No buses over thirty-five feet allowed."

I felt like a complete imbecile. It was so stressful, but I finally got the RV unwedged and was able to reattach the car and get out of there. It began to rain, which added to my angst from the entire experience.

I was desperate to find a place to park for the night. At the time, there were only three places that we knew of where we could safely park for the night:

1. Walmart
2. Cracker Barrel
3. A local church

Unfortunately, there were no Walmarts or Cracker Barrels in the small, eerie ghost-town area we were in, so a church parking lot was our only option. The GPS showed me that the closest church was only a few miles away. Unfortunately, we are never certain if a parking lot will be large enough to accommodate us until we show up there. The only time we typically park at a church lot on a Saturday night is if we are planning to attend that church on Sunday morning and if there is plenty of room for us to park without disrupting their parking for services.

Thankfully, a couple of minutes later, we were safely stopped at a church that was large enough for us to park. I could finally take a deep breath! Moments after I pulled into the lot, however, another car turned in right behind me. I was hoping and praying it wasn't the police. I was certain I had broken a few laws in the past hour or so. Thankfully, it was a woman who came to tell us that we probably didn't want to park in that particular neighborhood at night.

"Are you looking for a place to park?" she asked.

"Yes, we are," I responded.

"Well, you don't want to park here or anywhere near here. You'll wake up without tires if you stay parked here tonight!" she warned.

"Why don't you follow me back to my house? I've got a safe spot for you where you'll be able to plug in for the night. My husband and I have an RV parked in our driveway. We can easily move it over and will have plenty of room for yours if you're interested."

Interested?

Was she kidding?

We were beside ourselves with appreciation!

It turned out that since she and her husband were fellow RVers, they understood our plight. They generously offered to allow us to hook up so we would have power and would be safe until the morning. The couple was so trusting. They didn't know us from Adam, yet they were thoughtful enough to make sure we would be safe for the night.

We followed them back to their house. When we got there, we all introduced ourselves. They were Deby and Fred Broussard, the sweetest couple we'd met on the road so far. They moved their RV over so we could put our slides out, widening the total width inside our RV by several feet. With the slides in, it is difficult for everyone to comfortably sleep, so that was an added bonus.

When we woke up the next morning, I asked if they would mind if I took their picture. We had committed to trying our best to chronicle our trip—not just the places we were traveling to, but also the incredibly wonderful people we were meeting along the way.

As we were getting ready to depart, Fred asked if we were clear on where we were headed and did we have everything we needed for the trip? I assured him we were all set, especially in light of their already wonderful generosity.

It was obvious to Fred that we were still pretty new at all of this. We all waved good-bye as I shifted the RV into drive.

Just as I started to pull out, I heard the couple yell, "STOP!"

They were screaming as loud as they could for us to hold up. I wasn't sure why they wanted us to halt, but I threw the RV into PARK, opened the door, and asked, "What's going on?"

"You're still plugged in, Jay!" Fred screamed.

Oops! I had left my electrical cord plugged into their power source. We were such newbies! I was embarrassed and apologized for the mishap. Thankfully, Fred was a good sport and took it all in stride. Fred and Deby seemed amused by the whole ordeal.

That day was the creation of what we now refer to as our "take-off list." It is a checklist similar to what a pilot goes through before a plane is cleared for take-off. This would become an important tool while we were still getting used to the RV—that and a sign that Ben made reminding me that we have an antenna on the roof so I didn't knock it down...again!

It was fascinating to start discovering the kindness of strangers. We had lived our entire lives without recognizing just how giving people can be, even to people they don't know. Maybe it is because we didn't need anything; or perhaps it was because until we went to Africa, our lives had been primarily focused on ourselves. Whatever the reason, I can't recall many occasions where I felt like someone I'd never met completely had my back until then.

It's funny because when we had dubbed our journey the ARK Tour, we figured we'd be the ones demonstrating Acts of Random Kindness. Little did we know that this would be the first of many Acts of Random Kindness that would be bestowed on our family.

13 THERE'S A MOUSE IN OUR HOUSE

MAY 4, 2008
MEMPHIS, TENNESSEE

BETH» We left New Orleans and drove the whole day until 9:30 that night. We pulled into a Walmart parking lot fifty miles south of Memphis. Jay was exhausted from driving all day. I offered to drive several times since we left Atlanta, but Jay is the kind of guy who likes to be in control. He was the mighty captain of the ship! I knew he'd eventually relinquish some of the responsibility—at least I hoped he would.

Jay finally let me take the wheel for the first time on May 4. There had been so many little issues with the RV since we left, things breaking and going bad, which Jay simply didn't have the experience to handle with ease or a calm demeanor. While he was trying hard to give up and relinquish his need to be in charge all the time, there are just some things you can't control—like an unexpected infestation of mice!

JAY» A few days after we left Atlanta, I noticed some mouse droppings in the drawer where I kept my work files. I suspected we might have a rogue mouse running amok. I bought some mousetraps during our quick stop in Pensacola. I spread some peanut butter across the metal snap and set them in the drawer as well as around a couple of other areas I thought might be inlets for the critters. When I checked the traps later, the sly mouse (or mice) had licked them clean without losing his head. I couldn't believe it. Apparently, we were playing host to Mighty Mouse! The night we spent at Fred and Deby's in New Orleans, Mighty Mouse appeared again. Ben did some research on the Internet and discovered that mice like chocolate, so I decided to cram some chocolate chips into a trap and then set it, hoping this would work.

As we were heading to bed, I saw the mouse poke his head out of one of my cabinets, and then he quickly dashed under my bed. I completely freaked out. Yes, the captain of the ship—the alleged fearless leader of our family—is afraid of mice. I ran out of our bedroom screaming like a little schoolgirl. I sent Beth in with one of her shoes, but she didn't have any luck finding that sly mouse. I refused to sleep in that room until I knew the mouse was dead and gone. So, instead, I slept with Noah while Beth slept in the bedroom with the mouse. Beth was the only one who got a good night's sleep!

The next day we discovered that Mighty Mouse had eaten his last meal. You might say it was "death by chocolate"! Since then, we had a family of mice try to hitch a ride out of Iowa, but we allowed no stowaways! They were evacuated immediately with our weapon of choice… a Hershey bar!

By the time we left Atlanta for good, things in my business had taken a sharp turn for the worse. I was struggling to make a living. I was trying to keep up my business, but the market had quickly changed. To make matters worse, there were now more demands on my time, which distracted me from being on the phone, calling clients, and getting things done. Every little thing that went wrong with the RV became my sole responsibility.

And there was always something.

I remember talking to a friend who owned an RV about general maintenance before we bought ours. I should have known I would be in way over my head when he referred to his vehicle as "a tinkerer's toy."

I was never much of a handyman, so whenever something went wrong, it was a head-scratcher for me. I'd become angry, snappy, and crabby if

I couldn't figure out how to fix whatever was broken. I didn't want the added responsibility, especially while my business was in the tank. There were several days in the first few weeks, if not months, on the road where I seriously questioned if we had made the right decision. Beth and the kids loved the experience, while I was secretly dreaming of selling the RV.

We spent a month in Kansas City celebrating the marriage of our niece before leaving for the next leg of our trip. We purposely chose to spend the first several months of our trip visiting both our families and getting comfortable with our new lifestyle.

To be totally honest, we had gotten used to traveling around, sight-seeing, and doing lots of fun stuff along the way. We had set out to spend the bulk of our time serving others, but we hadn't really gotten around to doing much of that yet. We certainly had the intention and aspiration, but without realizing it, we had inadvertently put our mission to serve on the back burner.

BETH» Looking back on those first few months, I now realize how important they were and why we didn't jump into serving right away. Jay needed to learn and understand the intricacies of the RV before he could place his attention on anything else. We were brand-new at everything. We literally learned how to live on the road by being on the road. Laundry, shopping, even finding stores became an adventure, as if I were learning about these tasks for the very first time. When we had enough of being on vacation and began to live our lives on the road, we knew the transition had taken place and it was time to get to the task at hand—to serve.

14 ▸ AT A CROSSROADS

JULY 13–AUGUST 18, 2008
DENVER, COLORADO

JAY» We had been staying just outside Denver, Colorado, for two weeks or so trying to figure out what we should do next. We were thinking of making our way to California for the winter but were worried that it would be too expensive to get there. My business had all but dried up, which meant that money was tight. We were doing anything we could to avoid needless spending.

I asked the pastor of a local church if we could park in their lot until we had a plan. He said we could stay as long as we liked. He and his wife even invited us to their home for dinner so they could get to know us. They were super nice and turned out to be our kind of people. The pastor and I even went on a motorcycle ride together through the mountains.

During our stay in Denver we had learned of a church we wanted to visit called Red Rocks Church. We heard they were having an outdoor service in the park, so we pulled the RV up, introduced ourselves, and jumped right in to help. We began unloading water and ice, setting up tables and chairs, and doing a few other tasks. It was a great way to meet people, and they seemed to appreciate our help.

The more I thought about it, the more I began to question whether or not we should keep going on our journey. Since we were almost out of cash, I couldn't justify how we might be able to continue on. I was questioning everything. I wasn't sure what to do or where we should go. We contemplated staying in Colorado for the winter. I figured we could weatherproof the RV, which had no insulation to withstand a cold and snowy Colorado winter. Breckenridge seemed like a good choice for us to lie low for a while because it was extremely kid friendly and not as commercial as some of the other popular Colorado resorts. So we headed west until we got to the resort town just east of the Continental Divide.

When we got to Breckenridge, we had no clue where to park the RV; so we went to the local library and stayed in their parking lot until we could figure things out. The next morning, Beth took the kids inside the library to do their schooling for the day. While she was there, she met Jennifer Schrock, a woman from Michigan who also homeschooled her kids. Beth shared our story with Jennifer, who, after hearing about our family, was eager to come out and see the RV. Intrigued, she invited us to their rental vacation home for dinner that night to meet her husband, Troy, and their three kids—two girls Bekah's and Abigail's ages and a boy who is Noah's age.

Our families connected right away. We shared so many commonalities, especially our values and ethics. We also discovered we had some differences too. They attended a church where the women were required to wear head coverings, where men and women sit on opposite sides of the church, and where the women are not allowed to wear jewelry or makeup. They were extremely conservative, even for us; yet we completely enjoyed their company.

The next day, we were asked to leave the library parking lot. We had no place to go. When I checked around for other options, the cheapest RV park I could find was sixty dollars a night, significantly more than we could pay. Faced with having to leave the area, the Schrocks graciously offered to have our family stay in the fully furnished basement of their rental home for the week. We were hesitant to accept their offer at first because we didn't want to barge in on their vacation. They assured us their whole family was excited to host us.

We took the things we needed out of the RV and moved in for a week. The setup was perfect for us. There was a full kitchen, two bedrooms, and a central living area. We had an awesome week with their family, sharing meals, swapping homeschool ideas, going on a long hike, and engaging in deep discussion. It was interesting to meet another family who challenged our beliefs while we questioned theirs. Sometimes our discussions culminated with our families agreeing to disagree. Beth and I were more than intrigued by their way of life, and the more we engaged in lively conversations, the more it deepened our friendship with them. We found it extremely refreshing and healthy to be able to discuss these intimate issues in such an open way.

Beth and I really liked the vibe of Breckenridge. I thought about getting a job as a ski instructor at one of the local resorts or maybe driving a van for one of the hotels for the winter. I figured we could find a place to park and stay put for six months or so as a way to save up a little cash and figure out where we wanted to head to next.

While I was exploring our options, I had met a local guy who unknowingly added fuel to my already growing fear. He pointed to the mountains just west of where we were and said, "Things sure do get expensive on the other side of those mountains." My heart instantly dropped from my chest to the floor. Things would only get worse if we left and headed west—or so I believed. Vail, Aspen, Telluride, and onward to California—these were the places over the western slope known as the playground for the rich and famous. The farther west you travel, the more expensive it becomes. Gas, lodging, parking all seem to be higher on the other side of that ridge.

I couldn't shake this feeling that while spending the winter working and skiing in Breckenridge sounded great, it wasn't what God had planned for us. He was calling us to do something, even if we hadn't answered it yet. As much as I wanted to stay put, I knew in my heart and soul that we had to go. The only way we could move forward was for me to have the faith to break through my fear. It wasn't easy, but I believed so passionately that God would take care of us that I chose to place my destiny in His hands. I had to have the faith and courage that I was already on the ride, so I may as well fasten my seat belt and go along with it.

Here's the thing I now understand. You can believe in almost anything, but without faith and passion you will probably never act on it. If you don't step out in faith, you will never experience anything new. We didn't have a clue where we were going that day we left Atlanta. We just got into the RV and drove. And this time, despite my warranted fear, we saddled up and headed west.

That's faith in action.

BETH» In many ways I am extremely thankful to live without the overhead it takes to maintain a large house with an equally demanding yard to keep up. I do not miss all of the weeds that needed pulling and dealing with all of the superfluous stuff we've accumulated just because we had the extra space to store it!

It's true that most people live in a world that has become obsessed with stuff. Stuff to fill our houses, stuff to wear, stuff to play with, stuff to do, stuff to clean, stuff to drive, stuff to organize and put away, stuff for birthdays, holidays, events, and parties, stuff for sports, stuff to decorate, stuff to read, stuff to eat—it's too much stuff!

America is a society filled with mostly overworked, overspent, overcommitted, overextended, overweight, overbudget, overindulged, overtired, and overstressed people who lack peace, joy, contentment, calmness, and true richness in their lives. They have everything, yet nothing. From the outside looking in, they have a full life, yet lack a true life—leaving them empty, barren, and desolate.

When you live with excess, your appetite for stuff is never fully satisfied. Think about it this way: how many of you have all this stuff and still your kids complain they're bored with nothing to do? We spend a lifetime accumulating stuff only to get to the end of life and sell it or leave it for someone else to add to their stuff.

Since embarking on our journey, I can honestly say that I have learned that stuff doesn't bring fulfillment, happiness, or contentment. It does not bring joy. It complicates life. It crowds our space. It suffocates, stifles, preoccupies, lies, and distracts. When is enough, enough? You can't take any of these things with you when you die—not even a favorite pair of shoes or those expensive golf clubs.

Don't wait until it's too late to figure out that you would have lived your life differently if you could do it all over again. Live differently now!

15 THIS IS WHY WE CAME

SEPTEMBER 2008
SALT LAKE CITY, UTAH

As our oldest son, Ben, was preparing to enter high school in the fall, we started looking at schooling options that fit our lifestyle and his academic needs. After doing our due diligence, we found The American Academy, an online school that Ben could utilize for his curriculum. When we called the school for more information, we spoke to a man named Richard, who was the director of marketing for the program. We began explaining our situation to him, sharing our travels and our mission to serve, a message we knew was rooted in our Christian faith yet we believed speaks to everyone regardless of their religious beliefs. Richard, a Mormon, was extremely intrigued by our story. We shared our website with him so he could see who we are and told him we were going to continue on with our research but would call him the next day.

When we called Richard back to talk more about their online program, he said he had showed our site to his boss.

"We love what you're doing. We want to offer Ben a discount on our high school program." We thanked him for his generosity, and told him that we would need to discuss it because even their discounted rate made the program a stretch for us.

The following day, Richard called us to offer Ben a full scholarship.

We were stunned by his willingness to help us with our son's education. Richard invited us to come to Salt Lake City so we could all meet in person.

"While you're here, our marketing firm has a connection with a producer at the local Fox station. We ought to try and get you a segment on *Good Day Utah* so more people can hear about what your family is doing."

After we arrived, Richard set up that interview as well as a visit to the local Humane Society and the Salt Lake Rescue Mission.

Richard picked us up and we all served together at the Rescue Mission. First, we attended the chapel service they had each night before dinner and then served hot meals and helped clean up after the last person walked through the door. The people we served were used to picking up their own plates and putting them in the large black buckets after they finished their meals. On the day we were there, we wanted to clean up for them. They seemed to appreciate that small gesture. We used our cleaning as an opportunity to start up conversations with them.

All of us, including Noah, spent the day helping people who couldn't give us anything back in return except their appreciation. And we did it only to show love and appreciation for who they are as people. It was such a privilege for us to be there and show these men and women that someone cared about each of them.

This was the first time our family served together at a Rescue Mission. The service we had done prior to this involved working at a conference for high school students, setting up rooms, and cleaning up trash, along with helping at Red Rocks Church. This experience was different in that it caused something inside us to click, because although all service is important, we felt that showing love toward those who are hurting and broken and feeling like outcasts is especially powerful. All of a sudden, we began to have interactions with homeless men and women that reminded us of the people we met under the bridges back in Atlanta. When we started talking with them, listening as they shared their stories of how they got there, something just clicked.

This was why we came.

They were the people we were meant to meet and serve.

It took a man with a faith different from ours to kick-start our vision for service. Even if people don't agree on the fundamental principles of others' religious beliefs, there is a strong commonality among those with great faith, especially when it comes to serving. We are aware that what we believe is critically important. Christianity and the Mormon faith have some huge differences, but it was easy to discover that we share a common desire to serve and show God's love to people. Many Christians get stuck in a rut of believing something in their head but not acting on that faith and belief. As Christians, we can learn something from people from all walks of life and varying faiths. Sadly, many Christians will have nothing to do with those of other faiths. This is not the example that Jesus showed us. He loved everyone regardless of their faith or background.

After Salt Lake City, there was a change that none of us expected but perhaps we were finally ready for. We went from easing our way into service to full speed ahead. We continued our journey west so we could end up in California before the winter months hit.

Deciding where to go had become an organic decision. We knew where we wanted to eventually land, but the route we took to get there didn't matter all that much. What had become evidently clear after our service work in Salt Lake City was the need to do something as a family in all of the communities we visited from here on out, wherever we ended up.

It took us awhile to figure out how we would determine both where our services would be needed most and also which organizations would allow us to serve together as a family.

Because of our experiences under the bridges back in Atlanta, we knew those people feel like they are the forgotten outcasts of society that everyone ignores. Although it's not an easy place to go, we are most drawn to visiting the local homeless shelters or rescue missions, especially because so many others find those places difficult to be around. Sadly, there would always be a need there, but serving in that environment stretches us to embrace all people in all environments with love and appreciation—something they have all but given up on from others. We want to show them God's love and let them know they have not been forgotten—that somebody still cares about them. Sharing this experience as a family has the biggest impact of all. The kids are so touched by the collective feeling we get when we're serving those in need.

Local churches are also a great resource for whatever needs a community may have. Because of their local involvement, they are able to introduce and connect us with nonprofit organizations who are serving the poor and those in need.

We also discovered a nationwide service that can be accessed by dialing 211 on your phone. They will direct you to local senior centers, book banks, children's homes, and several other places with volunteer opportunities to anyone who is interested in offering a helping hand.

By the time we arrived in Boise, Idaho, we had done our research. We decided to contact local men's and women's shelters. When we arrived, we drove over to the men's shelter, but they told us the women's and children's shelter could really use our help, so we decided to serve there first.

BETH» I was really touched by the personal stories of the people we met at the women's and children's shelter. Too many times, people think that women end up in a shelter because they are drug addicts, alcoholics, or have mismanaged their finances. That is not always the case. Statistics have shown that more men are on the street by choice whereas women are there because of their circumstances.

What I discovered was that sometimes, especially now in these troubled economic times, good and honest women end up in a shelter because they've lost their jobs, their husbands divorced them, or they simply had no formal training or education to get a decent job to support their families. They end up on the street with their children, and they have absolutely nothing and no place to go.

Sometimes I think we all want to believe there is this chasm between the homeless, hungry, and us. The truth is, there isn't. Most Americans live so close to the edge. Statistics show that most are three paychecks away from being on the street. And it happens faster than you think.

I met one woman who told me she ended up at the shelter after having two babies from two different men who promised to take care of her but failed to keep their word. Her only choice was to find a local shelter to protect her children until they could get back on their feet. While I was talking with this woman, I realized she was a good-hearted woman who had made some poor choices and was also reaping the consequences of other people's actions. She was trying to provide for her children but was unable to make ends meet. She told me it didn't take long for her to lose her home and all of her belongings. She was doing the best she could before her circumstances changed and spiraled out of her control. That was how she ended up on the street. I tried to put myself in her shoes, wondering what life would have been like if Jay weren't the wonderful man he is. It could have been me in that shelter if I had ended up a single mom.

Of course, there are some women who are in shelters by choice. These are women who have been offered jobs and a way out through other opportunities but refuse to take the risk because they have a severe addiction and can't seem to break out of it to live a better life. These women are in need of help to recover before they can possibly think about working to support their families. There are ample programs available, and when they make the choice to step away from their lifestyle, the help is there for the taking.

What I understood that day was that everyone has something beautiful to offer. We all have a special gift, ability, or talent we bring into the world. We want to put ourselves on an equal playing field with others, but oftentimes our circumstances give us the belief that we are not. That negative mindset creates a self-fulfilling belief that you somehow belong where you are. This starts a cycle that keeps most people down and unable to get themselves out of difficult times.

I've had my own struggles with a negative mindset and thoughts. Having experienced the feelings of being stuck in a dark place makes me passionate about helping others who are struggling and showing them the truth that they are valued and special. I want to tell them they have so much to offer, that they're worthy and deserving of a better life. When people feel so beaten down and nothing seems to be working, they've got nowhere else to go but up. I know from personal experience because I've been there.

We make it a point to spend time getting to know the people we meet in the shelters. We want to develop relationships that are founded on truth and trust. We don't want to make it seem like we are merely around to feed them or to make ourselves feel good. We are there to help them feel better about their lives, despite the obvious setting. It is quite amazing to see how quickly most of the people we meet will open up to us. For the most part, they're eager to tell their stories because they feel safe and not judged. After some time and conversation, they can see that we are there because we care.

And we do care—deeply.

When we meet women who are so beaten down by their particular circumstances, we let them know that we believe in them and that we support and love them for who they are and who they are striving to become. I remember vividly being in the midst of my depression and having my dear friend Debbie spend hours on end talking with me and reminding me of the truth. When life was so dark and I believed that Jay and the kids would be better off without me, Debbie reminded me that my family loved, cared for, and needed me. Although it was hard to grasp, it was a comfort to know that someone believed in me, even though I didn't believe in myself.

The most incredible and moving experiences we've had have come from watching our children interact with the other children we meet in these situations. Watching Bekah hold a baby or Abigail play with some of the little girls is a wonderful sight.

We've worked hard to instill that type of unconditional love and acceptance into all of our children. Ben and Noah have such soft and kind hearts. They're not afraid to show their emotions by reaching out and hugging someone or placing an understanding hand on another's shoulder. It's wonderful to see our children show compassion and understanding.

When we left Boise, our intentions were to keep heading west, as the seasons were changing from summer to fall, which meant the air was cooler and the likelihood of encountering snow was greater. Getting stuck in a snowstorm would surely make our passage more challenging than we desired to endure. But despite our plan to continue west, we unexpectedly headed north. Something was guiding us to veer off the beaten path—again.

We headed up to a state park near McCall, Idaho, where we could park the RV for a few days and do some research on where we wanted to go next. We considered a few different churches before deciding on one to attend for services on Sunday morning.

We've attended church with all different affiliations, including Baptist, Assemblies of God, Methodist, Presbyterian, non-denominational, and everything in between. It doesn't matter to us which affiliation a church has as long as they're teaching out of the Bible. This is what we believe is the truth, so how these different congregations worship is irrelevant. In fact, we actually prefer to experience several different churches and how they worship throughout the country.

The most interesting aspect of experiencing a wide variety is the many ways there are to "do" church. We've attended services at some very conservative and strict churches, inner-city churches filled with mostly the homeless and those who may be down and out, as well as some unforgettable rocking, high-energy services. What we've found most inviting are those churches that stand for everyone—young, old, rich, poor, different backgrounds, and those from different nationalities. We enjoy experiencing a variety because it gets us away from the narrow mindset that there is only one way to worship.

We searched the Internet; and after reading over the website of the

Mountain Life Community Church, we were intrigued and chose to visit this small church nestled in the Central Idaho Mountains.

Within minutes of walking through the door, we were greeted by Dave and Linda Johnson, a wonderful couple who welcomed us like old friends. When we began sharing our journey with them, we could see their excitement for what we had set out to do.

"Where are you headed to next?" Dave asked.

"We were thinking of stopping in Coeur d'Alene on our way to Seattle. We've heard it is supposed to be gorgeous."

"I've got a house there. You can park in our driveway and have full access to our home if you'd like to. It's no problem at all if you need a place to hang your hat," Dave offered without missing a beat.

By this time we had learned to graciously accept these types of offers because we knew it was God working through the people we met to provide for us in ways we simply could never have imagined.

We struck up another conversation with one of the associate pastors who we didn't realize would be speaking later that morning. He asked where we were from and what we were doing on the road. We shared some of our stories of service with him, thinking nothing of it when we spoke.

Much to our surprise, when the pastor got up to speak, he asked our family to stand up as he introduced us to the entire congregation. He shared our journey and mission with the group, encouraging them to get involved in any possible way they could. We were slightly taken aback by this unexpected introduction, as this was the first time someone had called our work to the attention of others who would understand our vision for service. We didn't know what to expect. We certainly didn't anticipate the response we got.

"I've got a box of extra Bibles. Would you like to have those to give away on your trip?" one fellow asked.

It wasn't in our nature to hand out Bibles, but we graciously accepted them knowing that all things happen for a reason, and if someone was searching or in need, we'd be ready.

Another gentleman came up to us and offered his home in McCall. "I have a fully furnished cabin you can use while you're here. I usually rent it out, but no one is in it at the moment, so it's yours for the next couple of weeks if you want it."

We happily accepted his generous offer. A few days out of the RV sounded good to all of us. We were wowed by how gorgeous the cabin was. It was a fully decked-out home with a cabin feel that was extremely comfortable. It had four bedrooms, a large fireplace, and all of the comforts we could have asked for and then some.

Tom and Jo, another couple from the church, invited us to their house for dinner. They wanted to welcome us with a good old-fashioned home-cooked meal. They had four-wheelers, which they offered to us for some family fun. We had an absolute blast zipping around their property. Tom was a former music professor at a college and had a huge organ in his basement. He played a few songs for us, which was impressive and loads of fun.

Since we would be in McCall for a couple of weeks, we began looking at opportunities to keep our service momentum going. We asked around town about places we could visit or offer our help to. There weren't as many options in McCall as there were in bigger cities, but one thing we knew for certain was that there is always somewhere to serve.

We called the local senior center to ask if there was anything we could do for their facility. The woman we spoke to was a little bit aloof. She must have been uncertain about our motives or perhaps she had never received a call like ours before. She wasn't sure how to answer and asked if she could call us back.

When she returned the call, the woman at the center said they would appreciate it if our family would help them crush some cans.

That was it.

They wanted us to crush cans.

The woman's demeanor didn't change all that much when we arrived at the center. She wasn't warm or inviting. She still seemed confused by our offer to help—and then that we showed up. We tried to engage her in some friendly conversation, but she remained suspicious and distant.

We decided to have some fun with the task at hand, with each of us coming up with unique ways to crush the cans. Ben was jumping in the air, crushing six cans at a time. We could see his size thirteen feet were finally coming in handy. Noah tried to use his bare hands. We had a blast because we were all working together to accomplish a single goal.

As we crushed can after can, we wondered how much could a can crusher actually cost that they don't have one? When we finished the chore, we asked the woman from the center if they had thought of getting a can crusher. She explained that she really wanted one and had put in a request for it, but was told it wasn't in the budget.

We knew it couldn't be that expensive, so we drove down to the local hardware store to purchase a can crusher for the center before leaving town. Surprisingly, it was only $21.99. We were excited to surprise the senior center with something that for us was a very small gesture but for her was a dream come true.

When we drove back to the senior center to present the can crusher to them, the woman we had encountered earlier was moved by this small and simple act of kindness. Her demeanor completely changed as she hugged and thanked us over and over again as if we had just presented a large sum of money to the facility.

We were all unusually quiet as we drove away from the center that day. Our simple act of service left an indelible mark on all of us—even the woman who wasn't sure what to make of us, confirming, yet again, that even the smallest act of kindness can brighten anyone's day. Seeing the look on someone's face as they light up makes service gratifying and worthwhile.

WHEN YOU GIVE, YOU GET SO MUCH MORE IN RETURN

Once in a while, it feels like God wraps His arms around you, gives you a big cozy hug, and says, "I've got your back. I know when you're weary, and I know when you need rest. Stay close to Me, and I will be able to make that perfect flow happen in your life of giving and receiving."

We were beginning to see this happen in our lives over and over again where we would serve and pour ourselves out; but then we would suddenly find ourselves on the receiving end, being filled up by other people's kindness. There have been so many incredible and unexpected perks for our family along the way—gifts and gestures we simply never imagined when we started out. We never intended to have people reach out and give to us, but we are incredibly grateful for all of the kindness we have been given.

While it is easy for us to get swept away with serving others, we can never forget the people in our own home. To some degree, being selfish is part of human nature. We can give so much out there in the world and forget that we need to give of ourselves to our loved ones too. If we aren't serving our children, each other, and our family first, we have no business going out and giving our time and energy for other people. That would make us the worst kind of hypocrites.

We have our moments of selfishness, but we realize that it is critical that we show love within the walls of our own home or we will be hurting the people closest to us. Even if we've had a long day and feel as if there is nothing left to give, we cannot use that as an excuse to let each other down if there is a need to be filled.

This isn't something we always succeed at. Balance is something we continually strive for, and some days we completely miss that target. Unfortunately, at times, we can end up serving the leftovers to our own family. In a perfect world, we'd do this all right, all of the time. But we don't always succeed in hitting the mark.

It's important to remember that giving isn't just about going out in the world and doing good deeds. It's about seeing people as they are and offering them unconditional love and support. It is seeing a homeless man or woman as more than just "homeless." We once met a man who lived under the bridges in Atlanta. At first sight, he could have easily been mislabeled as uneducated or inept. We spent time talking to him and were astonished to hear that he had spent fourteen years in the military as a paratrooper. We would have never guessed he had such a rich and full previous life.

Everyone has a story to tell. Sure enough, we've all lived through some sort of pain, heartache, or experience that we've had to overcome or are possibly *still* overcoming. Giving is about sending out a message of hope when people feel so lost they've all but given up. It is about putting all judgments aside and seeing people through eyes of love and compassion. Someone once said to us that "it is impossible to judge someone once you've heard their story," and we have found this to be true.

When we set out to serve, we never imagined the rewards we'd get in return. There is nothing more fulfilling than leaving your own world of concerns and needs and looking for ways to brighten someone else's day. We repeatedly find that when we get our eyes off of ourselves and look to meet the needs of others—taking advantage of the opportunities that present themselves each and every day—happiness, joy, and contentment always follow. We have a more total sense of fulfillment now than we ever did before. While we may not be financially wealthy, we are rich beyond our wildest dreams.

Although it is sometimes hard to be on the receiving end, we have learned to accept people's generosity and their desire to support us. Just as we have experienced that it is more blessed to give than to receive, we know other people also experience a joy from giving. They feel wonderful, just as we do, using the gifts they have to enrich someone else's life. Not only have these gestures blown us away—they have shown us that we are not alone on this journey. Each time someone reaches out in thoughtfulness to us, we feel cared for, loved, and supported. All of the exhaustion and weariness are washed away and we are able to return to the journey feeling refreshed and renewed.

As rich as this journey has been, there have been times that it has been tempting to go back to living in the mainstream, settling down, and making a good living. To be completely honest, that would be a lot easier. But easier isn't always better. The true passion that fuels us is our love for God. If we don't serve Him, we are afraid of getting stagnant again. We don't want to waste our lives. We constantly think about eternity and how everything we do now will matter then.

We want to know that we were obedient to what He called us to do. Did we use the skills and talents He gave us to help others? We know that one day we will stand before Him, accountable for how we lived our lives. We realize that living in the mainstream isn't wrong, but we want to be able to say we gave it all we had. Like our friend Gerald Martinez from Albuquerque says, "I want to be loose change in the pocket of God that He can spend any way He wants."

CHALLENGE #6
When You Give, You Get So Much in Return

»» »» »» »» »» »» »» »» »» »» »» »» »» »» »» »» »» »» »» »»

One of the biggest perks that we've discovered in serving is that it brings joy. We always knew that it was more blessed to give than to receive, but we weren't prepared for the unbelievable, inexpressible amount of joy we received every time we served. It's common to think that when you serve, someone else's life will be changed, but inevitably you are the one who is changed and who receives more in the end. Luke 6:38 says, "Give, and it will be given to you. A good measure, pressed down, shaken together, and running over, will be poured into your lap. For with the measure you use, it will be measured to you."

We've experienced this principle firsthand. The more we've given and poured out, the more we've received. One of the things we've learned is that the joy of giving isn't just for us, for those with means, or for those who live in the suburbs; it's for everyone. We now invite the people we serve to serve with us so they can also experience the joy of giving.

At times it can be tempting to give to those who can give back to us; however, we've found that there is greater joy in giving to those who have no way to repay you. In Luke 14:12 Jesus says, "'When you give a luncheon or dinner, do not invite your friends, your brothers or relatives or your rich neighbors; if you do, they may invite you back and so you will be repaid. But when you give a banquet, invite the poor, the crippled, the lame, the blind and you will be blessed. Although they can't repay you, you will be repaid at the resurrection of the righteous.'"

» How strong is our love for others if it's always given to those who already love us?

» With whom can you step out and experience the joy of giving?

We challenge you to give to those who can't repay you and then be ready to receive much more than you give.

17 THE LOECKEN FAMILY MISSION

OCTOBER 25, 2008
PORTLAND, OREGON

JAY» My worst fears of heading west were coming true. The closer to California we got, the more expensive everything became. Up to this point, we had gotten by financially due in large part to the generosity of others who were eager and delighted in providing places to stay and other provisions to us along the way. We never asked for handouts, but people came out of the woodwork at just the right time to meet real needs that we had.

One huge surprise came while we were on our way to Portland, Oregon. We were searching online for RV parks near Mount St. Helens. We called a place named Toutle River RV Park. Since they were brand-new and not yet officially opened for business, the state would not allow them to charge. They let us park there for a full week, absolutely free. It generally costs between $500 and $800 per month to park an RV. It all depends on the location and facility. If you pay by the night, it can be as little as $20 or as high as $50 or $60 and sometimes even $100 a night—more money than we could afford at any price because we didn't want to spend what little money we had on parking.

I was doing everything I could think of to drum up business from the road; but times were tough, and business was scarce for everyone in the mortgage industry. Despite all my efforts, our finances were drying up.

Although our financial needs were greatly lessened by moving into an RV, we still had the expenses of parking, gas, food, clothing, RV expenses and maintenance, insurance, cell phones, and Internet access. I have always made sure that I meet our family needs before meeting anyone else's. There was nothing Beth and I weren't willing to do to make sure we took care of those needs every single day. We were willing to dig ditches, paint houses, or whatever was necessary to bring in some quick extra cash.

With all of the homes we had lived in and fixed up, we had become skilled painters; and we thought we might be able to drum up some business and make a little quick cash before leaving Coeur d'Alene, Idaho. We were going to call it J&B's Painting Service. We made up fliers to hand out around town that explained our family's mission and that we'd only be available for a couple of weeks.

Okay—looking back, it's easy to understand why no one wanted to hire us. After all, who was going to trust us knowing we'd be leaving in a couple of weeks! We were just trying to be creative to figure out a way to make some money, but our marketing strategy wasn't all that well thought out on that particular venture. We wanted to continue the journey we were on and were willing to do whatever it took to keep our dream alive.

To help supplement my income as a loan officer, I had taken a job selling a follow-up system to mortgage companies that loan officers could use as a way to keep up with their clients. Unfortunately it took time to build my client base. I was working fifty hours a week at both jobs and was still barely making any income. I regularly had to dip into our savings to keep our heads above water. By the time we got to Portland, Oregon, I was only bringing in $300 to $400 a month in residual income by selling the follow-up system. It was then that Beth and I had to reevaluate what we really wanted to pursue because I was rarely available for the family, and we were slowly watching our dream of serving slip through our fingertips.

When we got to Portland, Oregon, someone told us about a woman named Danielle Swope who had developed a program called The Children's Book Bank. Her organization makes books available to disadvantaged kids. Danielle collects used books, cleans them up, and allows children from the area to access them at the local book bank.

Danielle had been a Teach for America high school teacher in rural North Carolina from 1991 to 1993. She experienced how students from poor families struggled to succeed in school. Interestingly, the most significant obstacle she faced teaching math was that her students' reading skills were terribly limited. The high school in which she taught was not under equipped, understaffed, or underfunded. After a few weeks on the job, it became clear to Danielle that the lack of resources at home and the lack of preparedness going into kindergarten were the two biggest contributing factors to the children's lack of fundamental literacy skills on which their entire future education would be built. When Danielle recognized this problem for her students, she knew she had to act and do something to change the statistics.

For children who live in or slightly above the poverty level, literacy development is hampered by the scarcity of books available in their homes and schools. The ratio of books to children in middle-class homes is thirteen books for every one child. Sadly, the ratio of books to children in low-income homes is one book to three hundred children.

Danielle's life purpose and mission had become focused on getting more books into the hands and homes of young children who might not otherwise have books of their own.

We were blown away by her thoughtful inspiration and offered our services to help out by sprucing up and sorting through the donated books for low-income preschool children in the Portland area. We thoroughly enjoyed our time helping Danielle as we realized the books we were organizing could change many children's lives.

Much to our surprise, the local ABC affiliate heard about us being in town and decided to do a story on our family. We hadn't had much publicity or done more than a couple of interviews, so it was thrilling and scary at the same time. We were never out to seek attention—but it was beginning to come. We strongly felt that any attention we received should get directed toward God because He is the main story and we are simply average people just trying to make a difference. We also knew there were many other people out there in the world who tirelessly serve—those people are due the thanks and recognition a lot more than we are. Still, the media likes a good story; and for whatever reason, they were beginning to grab onto ours.

Later that night as we watched the local news, the anchor turned to her co-anchor and said, "This family is going out there to do acts of random kindness, and now they're inspiring other people to do the same thing."

This statement was another real *aha* moment because up until then it hadn't really hit us that we could or would inspire others to follow in our footsteps.

Great idea! we thought. It hit us like a ton of bricks that we had a bigger opportunity at our feet than we had realized. A light bulb went off. We were up for hours talking about ways we could inspire others.

We had been praying and seeking God for months, asking Him why He had led us on this journey. We were confident He led us out of Atlanta for a greater purpose—we just weren't completely sure what that was, but it was becoming clearer each day.

JAY» Since my business was slow, I had spent a lot of time thinking and praying about a new direction. I wanted to do something with my life that tapped into my deepest passions. Something that I could vigorously pursue that fit my personality and abilities. But most of all, I wanted it to be something that involved the whole family. In a way, I was looking to create a family business.

We've always tried to teach our children that you have to give yourself fully to whatever you do in order to achieve great results. You can't do something here and there and expect to have the same effect. If we fully dedicated ourselves to serving, it was certainly within our reach to make a life-changing impact in the lives of others. At that point, I decided to let go of the part-time job of selling the follow-up system to mortgage companies and keep my full-time job as a mortgage broker to pursue the ARK Tour and better immerse myself in inspiring others to serve.

While I felt like we were creating something very special with the work we were doing, it was pretty obvious that we were also flying by the seat of our pants. We had set out to make a difference in other people's lives, but how we were going about it was as haphazard as our itinerary. One day we were heading west and the next day north. The more we extended ourselves through acts of random kindness, the bigger the effect it had on our family. Every experience not only brought us closer but also made an impression on those we served.

It was time to sit down with the family and map out our real mission. The only way I knew how to make that happen was to create the official Loecken Family Mission Statement.

Now, if you saw the movie *Jerry McGuire,* you are aware that it was his need to create a mission statement that changed the course of his life forever. Jerry was a sports agent who wanted to get away from the sleazy aspects of his business by aiming to do things with integrity and a conscience. Some argued it was the best thing that ever happened to the guy, while others questioned his honesty, integrity, and fearlessness to speak his truth. An honest sports agent didn't seem to be what the field was looking for. After losing his job and starting his business, Jerry struggled along until he was able to find a balance between the sports world and the ideal world he imagined when creating his mission.

That storyline was beginning to sound all too familiar!

I likewise felt that we needed to create a mission statement so we were all on the same page about what we were doing and why.

Beth, the kids, and I sat around the kitchen table in the RV and came up with our family mission statement, which became a defining moment for all of us because it clearly spelled out the expectations we had for ourselves and the standard to which we would now expect to be held. This is what we came up with for our family mission statement:

> *The Loecken family mission is to, first, love God with all of our heart, soul, mind, and strength; and then to love each other by doing acts of random kindness in our own family first and then for others.*

These guiding words laid the foundation upon which everything else would be built as we moved forward. Creating this statement wasn't hard. It came directly from Jesus in Matthew 23:37–39. Loving God and loving your neighbor as yourself are the two most important commandments in the Bible. The next step was to create a mission statement for our work in traveling with a purpose:

> *The ARK Tour mission is to motivate, inspire, and encourage families to serve together by doing acts of random kindness wherever they are.*

While we worked on ironing out the details on new ways to put these plans into action, we spent the bulk of our time in Portland looking for outlets and areas where we could continue to serve.

We heard about a local shelter that provided more than two hundred hot meals to homeless people every Sunday. The group that organized the food drive had no particular religious affiliation. They were just people who cared about helping people. We went down to the shelter and served food in the line, hoping we could connect with these men and women.

Sometime that afternoon it occurred to me that what we essentially do is pop in and out of these situations whenever we can. Yet all around us there are people who tirelessly serve every single day. They're thoughtful, loving, and kind-hearted people who give back without any acknowledgments, accolades, pats on the back, or media attention. These are the unsung true heroes out there helping and inspiring people. They are the real servants in the world, sacrificing for the welfare of others. I decided to create a section on our website dedicated to telling their stories and highlighting the work they do. I also included other people we met along the way, whose stories were unique and inspiring.

Ben and I had been reading a book together called *Do Hard Things,* by Alex and Brett Harris. We often read books together that we later discussed from a father-son/man-to-man perspective. I was so intrigued by the book that I e-mailed the authors. I wanted to pick their brains on what they were doing and about their experience writing a book. When they e-mailed me back, they explained that they were in school on the East Coast, but their dad was a pastor at a church in Portland, called Household of Faith Community Church. It is a family-integrated church, which means the whole family attends church together instead of a typical setting where children are separated into Sunday school classes or small groups. We thought that idea was really unique so we attended their service to see what they were all about.

Most of the church families had six or seven kids, and sometimes more. This made us feel like a small family for the first time in years, and it tugged at Beth's heart to fulfill her dream of having eight to ten children. She always wanted a big family and was hopeful we'd someday meet that desire. However, our circumstances were limiting my desire to bring another child into the world, at least for the time being.

We were touched by the warm reception we received at the Household of Faith Community Church, with several members of the church coming over to introduce themselves and welcome us to their congregation. After services, we met Terry Neese, a man who shared with us that he had come out of an addicted lifestyle and, until recently, was living homeless for three years. After attending a support program at the Portland Rescue Mission and through his involvement at the Household of Faith Community Church, Terry's life had become stable. He was finally off the streets and headed in a positive direction.

Terry asked us if we had any needs. He was persistent in his desire to do something for us. We struggled with being honest because we knew he was getting his life back together. We were humbled because we felt like we should have been the ones to offer to help him. Still, we were floored by his desire to help us. He told us he wanted to stop by the RV before we left to give us something. When he did, we invited him in so we could get to know him better. We loved hearing his story of the challenges he overcame and how he persevered through tough times.

"I want you to have this" Terry said as he handed me a fist full of twenties.

We knew Terry didn't have much to his name and that he was just getting back on his feet, so we graciously thanked him but explained we couldn't accept his generous gift.

"I want to do this for you and your family." We could see the sincerity in his eyes as tears began to well up in ours. We continued sharing our stories with one another and ended up talking for hours. We asked him to tell us about his experiences living on the streets. We were curious to know what people need when they're living in that difficult situation.

"You want to know what they really need? Socks! Especially if you live here in Portland, because if your feet get cold your whole body begins to shiver." His answer was surprising, yet totally intriguing.

"Another thing they can use is an envelope with a postage stamp already attached, a pen, and some paper so they can write a letter to a loved one." He explained to us that oftentimes, homeless people want to make contact with their families or someone important to them, but they don't have access. They have no phone and no money to make a call or simply buy a stamp to mail a letter. It was so basic and fundamental and something we would never have thought of because we've never lived on the street.

After we said our good-byes, we unrolled the cash he'd handed to us. It was $100! We suddenly knew what to do with the money he'd given to us. We would purchase socks, paper, envelopes, and stamps and put together homeless care packages we could pass out. We were so excited about this idea that we began to think of other things we could add to the bags, including rain ponchos, wet wipes, and granola bars.

After fourteen rainy days (and to be totally fair, four almost sunny ones) we left Portland and headed south to Crescent City, California. When we arrived, we eagerly went shopping for the needed items, even thinking of more goodies we could add to the bags, including a toothbrush and toothpaste, a comb, a mirror, and deodorant.

With the hundred dollars, we were able to put together twenty-five packages. We put a handwritten note inside each one that simply read, "You are not forgotten. God loves you and so do we." We wanted the recipients to know that someone cared and they were not forgotten people.

We keep the packages in our car and each time we see someone standing on a corner holding a sign or anyone who is obviously homeless, we hand them a package. It is heartwarming to see their reaction when they discover a fresh, clean pair of socks in the bag. It is just a small token, but it gives us the opportunity to share a moment with these people, to look at them in the eyes and say, "We are thinking about you."

We have friends who believe that if someone asks you for money, you should always give whatever you can. We have always struggled with that philosophy because we don't want to create dependency. We usually turn around someone's request for a handout by asking, "Are you hungry? We will buy you a hot meal," but we've always been pretty adamant about not handing out money in these types of situations because there is no control over how they'll end up using it. There have been times we've made exceptions, where something in our gut told us money was the right thing to give.

Many panhandlers use the money you give them to get their next fix or to buy a six-pack at the local liquor store. While this is not true of every person who asks for money, it happens more than you would think it does. When people give money, it sometimes exacerbates the problem instead of helping. The exchange of money becomes a transaction between those who give and the person who receives. The ones giving feel good about themselves because they feel like they did a good deed, and the homeless people get what they want so they can continue in their destructive habits.

When we look to serve those in need, it should be more about a relationship than a transaction. Take the time to not only buy someone on the streets a meal but actually sit down and eat with them to learn about their lives. Ask them what they are good at. Perhaps you can volunteer at a homeless shelter so you can get to know the people there by name. The reality is that relationships are messy, and we simply don't want to take the time to build them, especially with someone who is so different than we are.

A homeless person needs a relationship with someone more than he needs some spare change. Panhandlers continue to beg and ask for money because it is easy and effective. When we take the path of least resistance to alleviate our guilt rather than pursuing the more difficult path of a relationship, we are in danger of causing more harm than good. We don't want you to ignore the plight of someone in need, but it's important that we be prayerful and thoughtful in how we interact with people in distressed situations.

Giving something like the care packages we created meant we could rest easy knowing we had helped in some small way without enabling a possible addiction.

This experience has been very powerful for the kids too. Abigail is especially aware of people on the street when we are driving.

"We have to turn around!" she says, pointing toward someone she spotted a couple of blocks back.

And we do.

Even if we can't get to the person because of traffic or one-way streets, we will park on the side of the road, get out, and often hop a median to get the bag to them. It's a really powerful thing to walk up to a man digging through a trash bin, look at him right in the eyes, and say, "Here you go. You are not forgotten. God loves you and so do I." Hearing a soft thank you or seeing tears well up is enough to melt even the toughest heart.

Thanks to Terry and his remarkable insights, we were able to create something that means so much to others that didn't cost a lot of money and is simple to give away. Terry was our greatest inspiration to create the homeless care packages because he is a perfect example of a life that has been changed because of the power of God and kindness that other people have shown to him.

After we got to Crescent City, I reached out to a friend from Atlanta, John Turner, who was now living in Southern California and had written several books. Along the way, people have told us that we should write a book about our journey, but we didn't have a clue how to write or publish a book. I decided to call John to tell him about our work and to see if he could give me some insight.

Surprisingly, he had just gotten back from speaking at a church in Santa Rosa where he mentioned our family in his message. The name of the church was New Vintage, and it was designed for people who were sick and tired of church. It was supposed to be really hip and cool, which sounded like a place we'd like to experience for ourselves. John said he shared a message with the group about a guy who finds Jesus and says, "What must I do?"

"Sell everything you have," Jesus said.

He spoke to the congregation about our family as a modern-day example of that message. After talking it over, he thought it would be wild if we stopped at the church. We were both baffled at the perfect timing of all of this. John connected me with Andy VomSteeg, the pastor of the church, so we could talk with him and get his thoughts on our family visiting his church. Andy said we could park the RV overnight in their parking lot and that he'd be happy to offer us a few minutes to speak at each of their three services.

We headed down to Santa Rosa. After a white-knuckle drive in the dark through the Redwoods of California, we found ourselves in a small parking lot being greeting by Andy and his wife, Kelli. It was late, so after we introduced ourselves, we quickly parked the RV and hooked up to their water and electricity. Even though they were extremely limited on space, Andy wanted us to park in the small lot closest to the entrance for effect.

When Andy got up to speak, he looked out in the crowd and said, "I'd like to know who parked their RV in our lot today."

Everyone looked around wondering who on earth would be that inconsiderate to take up seven parking spots with such limited space. We chuckled to ourselves at Andy's humor. He proceeded to introduce us to the perplexed crowd.

"Most of you probably think pastors tell stories they pull out of thin air to miraculously fit their message on any given day. And some of you may even wonder if they are actually true," Andy said.

"Well, if you were here a week ago, you might recall hearing about a family that had sold everything they owned to go out on the road and serve God."

Several heads nodded in response, recognizing the story the pastor was sharing.

"Well, here they are!" He introduced our family, and then we all went on stage to briefly share our story. The audience seemed genuinely surprised and happy to see us there and to listen to our story.

After the service, Andy and Kelli invited us out to dinner, where we shared more of our background with them as well as our passion for inspiring families to serve.

"What are you doing next weekend?" he asked.

Truth be told, we didn't have any plans.

"Would you consider coming back and speaking at all three of our services?" We were thrilled for the opportunity to share our life stories, including the trials and hardships we had been through. In total, that meant we would be addressing around a thousand people or more on that following Saturday and Sunday.

The following week, after we finished speaking, lines of people gathered around us to share their stories with us—especially with Beth, who had been so open and real about the abuses and losses she had suffered as a young girl. Several women wanted to talk to Beth alone, which meant she touched some part of their heart with her story.

As we were nearing the door to leave, a woman named Cindy told us she and her husband, Bob, owned a hot air balloon company based out of Napa. She offered to take the entire family up for a ride. This was something that was definitely on our bucket list, but we could never justify the expense to actually do it. We delightedly accepted her kind and generous offer.

After expressing a desire to get T-shirts printed, someone told us about a guy named Mark who owned a screen-printing and embroidery business who had done some work for the church. We contacted him and then went to his office and screen-printing facility. We struck up a conversation where we told him about our mission. He immediately offered to print up T-shirts with the ARK Tour on them.

When Mark shared his story, he explained that he had done some time in San Quentin prison on a tax issue. When he got out, he decided to start his own T-shirt business. He has no sales force but rather he gives T-shirts away as part of his marketing. And if there's a cause he believes in, he'll print up T-shirts for them free of charge. He said he loved our story and was inspired by the work we were doing. He had some extra inventory of white T-shirts that he printed our logo on the front and VOLUNTEER on the back so we could wear them whenever we were serving. We were taken aback by his kindness.

People from New Vintage welcomed us with open arms for the entire time we were in the area. They gave us loaves of bread, donuts, and even an invitation to go wine tasting at some of the wineries in nearby Sonoma. We even experienced an authentic Ethiopian meal. Our hostess was from Africa and shared her culture with us by preparing a full, ten-course, traditional spread. None of the food looked familiar to us, but it was all delicious. We ate the entire meal with our fingers, which is quite traditional for her culture but was very unusual for us. The woman who welcomed us into her home had very little. She didn't have a car or a lot of furniture, but somehow she had the desire to give to us by preparing an unforgettable meal for our entire family. This type of giving was overwhelming, as we had never felt this welcome in any one place. We were completely blown away by the friendliness and generosity of their congregation.

Several folks asked Andy if we would be available the next week to talk further about some of the hurts and past experiences we had spoken about in church. We couldn't ignore the desire these people had to talk to us, so we agreed to stay. We spent the week listening to people and sharing our experiences with the hope of helping them get through whatever crisis they were battling at the moment.

As the week continued, Beth began receiving e-mails from people who wanted to share their stories with her. They wrote because they weren't able to meet with us for one reason or another, yet they still wanted us to hear their challenging yet uplifting stories. They felt a deep connection with Beth and easily poured their hearts out on the page to her.

In the meantime, I had been seeking uplifting stories that I could add to our website as a tool to help inspire others. We read a letter from a man whose wife had battled cancer for ten years who decided to start a camp for children with cancer to help them get through the experience.

Another man wrote to tell us about his wife, who was a basketball coach to disadvantaged kids. She selflessly gave of herself to her students, but had a soft spot for one girl in particular. She loved this young lady like she was her own child. She became a second mom to her, took her in, and mentored her in everyday life. One day, the coach was stunned to learn she was in dire need of a new kidney. If she didn't get one, she would die. The young girl she had spent so much time with over the years was a perfect match to be a donor, a gesture that would ultimately save her life.

And finally, we heard from a retired businessman who made a choice to spend his free time going to schools to help disadvantaged kids instead of playing golf with his buddies every day. He tutors and mentors the young kids. I was especially touched by his story because he was a great example of someone who was choosing to use his God-given gifts to help others in his retirement as opposed to living only for himself.

This gentleman gave us a lot to think about for years to come— which brought us back around to a simple yet powerful message. God wants us to use our unique talents and gifts to help others. He has given each of us something special. The goal is to discovers yours and then use it to benefit others.

》》》》》

We were lucky enough to spend our first Thanksgiving on the road in Santa Rosa. We kicked off the day by taking the hot air balloon ride over the valley. The view was breathtaking! It was the most amazing and fantastic experience. As we left the earth and gently floated up, we saw beautiful farms and land from high above. The heat from the flames that propel the balloon upward is intense. The sound is louder than you might expect too, but once you're airborne and in the airstream, it's the most peaceful and serene experience any of us have ever had.

After our flight, Cindy, the owner of the balloon company, treated us to an amazing breakfast buffet. The flight was the most wonderful way to take a few minutes and think about how blessed our lives had become. We had so much to be grateful for this Thanksgiving.

Toward the end of our first week in Santa Rosa, we met the Matthews family, who invited us to stay at their ranch just outside of town. They said we could park the RV next to their house and stay for as long as we'd like.

Our intention was to only stay in Santa Rosa for a week, but that time flew by so fast. Beth and I both felt our work there wasn't finished. After talking it through, we wanted to stay and do more for the people we had met since arriving a week or so earlier. We decided to take the Matthews up on their very kind and generous offer.

When we arrived at the ranch, they actually had to cut down branches off their trees so we could get the RV into their driveway. And even though it was a tight squeeze, we made it.

The Matthews introduced us to Felicia, their teenage daughter who had been struggling with several issues. Beth was able to spend some quality time with her over the course of the two extra weeks we were at their home. She counseled this young lady almost daily. They took long walks where they talked about life and the reasons she might be hurting.

The Matthews told us their daughter was adopted and had suffered some abuse in her early life.

Beth was able to relate to her, having been through trauma and abuse herself. The Matthews loved their daughter but weren't equipped with the skills to handle what she was going through. She had gotten into some trouble along the way, leaving her parents at a crossroads on what to do. Although Felicia was in counseling, she was feeling so alone. Her family loved her but they couldn't understand how she was feeling because they hadn't been through those kinds of experiences.

All Beth did was offer Felicia a sympathetic ear whenever she felt the need to talk and offered her some advice from someone who had been through similar things as she had been through. The young woman found so much strength in hearing someone else talk about getting through those times. She thought she'd be stuck in that dark place forever. Beth assured her that wouldn't be the case. We both found a lot of comfort in knowing she would be okay.

The timing of our arrival into the Matthews' lives was nothing short of divine. Their daughter needed someone to talk to who could relate to what she was going through without making her feel judged or insecure. Beth was the perfect person for that.

We can't even begin to thank the Matthews family for their incredible generosity to us for the two weeks we stayed with them. They let us take over their driveway and allowed us to sketch off of their water and electricity. We had an incredible time getting to know their whole family. We left a part of our hearts with them when we had to say good-bye.

BETH» Meeting fun, unique, interesting, and amazing people everywhere we go is one of the many perks of traveling full time. Whenever we arrive in a new location, we are walking into the unknown. We meet strangers who quickly become friends. We have discovered that since our time in each location is somewhat limited, our lives often meld with theirs in a matter of days. It's truly a beautiful experience, one that we honor and cherish. Yet each time we settle in, we find it difficult to once again leave and head back out into the unknown.

When it comes time to pack up and leave a location, it is hard on all of us. It usually brings tears to our eyes. Although it is painful to leave, we also have a deep peace knowing that we are doing what we are supposed to be doing. That helps all of us tremendously because we never get this sense that we are supposed to stay in a specific area once our work is done. We all feel ready to go when the time comes, but it's just hard to say good-bye to people you've become close with.

With every departure, we know there is another adventure that lies ahead. We are inspired and motivated to press on because we know we will meet new people whom we will intersect with and who will bring growth and fullness to our lives. Every single place we've been has given us something to take with us to our next stop. Maybe it's a lesson, a story, or a fond memory of what we experienced. The transient lifestyle has become the cycle of our life these days, one that has brought each of us closer to one another and, more so, even closer to God.

18 UNIFIED FAMILIES REFLECT GOD'S PERFECT RELATIONSHIP WITH HIMSELF

BETH» There are so many positives we've shared on the road together as a family. I love that we are close and experiencing life as a family unit. When we lived in Atlanta, we were usually going in different directions—just passing each other along the way. We were fairly typical of most busy American families that way. Now, we do almost everything together. One thing that has had the most significant effect on our family is serving together. I have seen this bring us closer as we are all working side by side, loving others in a very physical and practical way. It's powerful.

What we've also noticed is that the people we help are greatly moved by seeing a family serving together. They comment on it often and it seems to touch them in a special way. I'm never quite sure if it's because they feel the warmth and acceptance radiating from the kids or if it's because of the fact that we choose to bring our kids into settings that many would find unsafe and they feel moved by our trust. Whatever the reason, we have seen the power that it has had—both to those we serve and to our family.

You might think that the endless hours we spend together now would drive us all crazy—which, at times, it does—but I can honestly say that we enjoy being together. We actually enjoy each other's company and are genuinely interested and involved in each other's day-to-day lives.

WHAT IS THE HARDEST THING OR BIGGEST CHALLENGE ABOUT BEING ON THE ROAD?

》》》》》》》》》》》》》》》》》》》》》》》》》》》》》》》》》》

BEN »» The biggest challenge about being on the road is the space aspect and not being able to have a place to get away. The second would have to be arriving at a place, meeting new friends, and then in two months having to pack up again and leave the friends that I had just made and was getting connected with. I am grateful that I am able to keep up with most of my friends on Facebook and Twitter. Both have been a great tool to help me stay connected.

BEKAH »» The hardest thing about being on the road is leaving your friends. You meet new people all the time, and then you have to leave them. Then at the next place, you have to meet new people again. It's like you're always the new kid. But then you have so many friends all over the country! Another challenge is not having a lot of space. We only have one shower and one toilet for all six of us! That is a challenge when we are all getting ready for church!

ABIGAIL »» The hardest or biggest challenge for me is setting up my bed—unfolding it, filling it up with air, and putting the comforters on it. Another one for me would be to have to fit in at new churches every few months. I also don't like it when I want to get just some "alone time" or privacy—but think about it, we live in a motor home with six people and a dog. There isn't much room to have that certain space that I need. My only get away place is our car, which is sometimes occupied by my other siblings who are feeling the same much-needed privacy time that I feel.

NOAH »» It's kind of challenging because you're kind of smooshed and you run into people because it's so small.

As wonderful as it is, being mobile full time definitely comes with its share of challenges! Sometimes we get exhausted and need time to pull away. I definitely miss taking hot baths, watching movies on our old flat screen, having a yard for the kids to play in, and space.

Yes, space.

There's not a lot of room to have a moment alone when you share such tiny quarters with five other people! I crave solitude—as I think we all do. Being by myself recharges my batteries. I like to take walks, and that helps me to get some time alone; but it's rare to get it in the RV.

When six people live together in an RV, there is no hiding emotion. You can't get away with anything! So, if one of the children is sulking, we all know it. This is why we do our best not to let negative feelings fester. If the kids are bickering—and let's face it, they do—no one is running into their bedroom and shutting a door until they cool off. It's definitely a challenge to get away with having an attitude or getting into an argument in this amount of space.

Whenever there's a conflict, we have to immediately work things out. Hurt or angry feelings can't be swept under the rug. Many people shove life's little annoyances under the rug so they don't have to deal with them. If you do that, eventually those little things become big problems; and before you know it, things are on the verge of exploding.

We've learned to talk about things before they become bigger issues, apologizing and offering forgiveness when needed. If we don't, it affects everyone else's attitude; and before you know it, we've got a bus full of grouchy people with nowhere to go.

Thankfully, we had some important experience on how to do life together before we hit the road. We knew how to work out our problems and differences, which has made it a little easier to tackle issues in the confines of the RV. Even so, the tight space has taught us all to have more patience and understanding for one another. Being in each other's way is a common problem, and sometimes just trying to get into the bathroom to brush your teeth can become cause for frustration.

It may take a little diversion like going for a walk or taking a drive to clear our heads because, often, that's what's needed to get past it. Occasionally, an apology is all that's needed—while other times, as most parents of teenagers know, you just need your space.

Teenagers need to get away every so often too, and that's completely understandable. Now and then, the kids will go into the car to read or just hang out. If no one else is using the back bedroom, they will ask if they can be alone to read. Ben also likes to sit in the back room and play guitar, which is his favorite way to unwind and relax.

Our kids also enjoy getting together with friends they've met on the road and doing things without their siblings and parents tagging along. We usually try to give each of our children the opportunity to enjoy some independence whenever we can.

One of the things we have always emphasized to our children is to never treat someone else better than you do your sibling. We expect our kids to be good friends with each other and to treat one another with love and respect. We communicate and leave nothing undone. No one goes to bed with anger in his or her heart.

Jay and I have also made it a point to carve out some alone time together as our way of keeping our relationship close. We enjoy going out on dates or getting together with other couples while the kids stay home. We do date night almost every Friday evening, which has been our routine since we were first married. We felt it was even more important to keep that tradition going on the road. We both feel it is vital to our relationship to carve out some alone time together. It's sacred time for us. Date night isn't terribly negotiable. Unless there is something that cannot be rescheduled, we plan everything around knowing Jay and I are together on Friday nights. We may choose to combine our date night with seeing friends by spending some alone time together prior to meeting up with other couples, but we always make it a point to set that time aside for ourselves so we don't disconnect with one another.

Even though we live in a small space, we can sometimes still find our lives passing like two ships in the night. Jay has projects he is working on during the day, along with meeting people and figuring out our next locale, while I've got my world with the kids, homeschooling, and doing different activities with them. We might go days without sharing what's happening in each of our lives. Date night creates an environment where we can reconnect, which helps our relationship stay close. We'll sometimes go on motorcycle rides and end up at a park, a lake, or even a bookstore where we can just sit and talk.

Since our finances are usually fairly tight, we may go out and share a meal together. Frequently, we've found that the portions in many restaurants are large enough for two people anyway, and we end up completely satisfied. Every now and then we might splurge on a movie or get dessert, but those aren't usually in our budget so they've become a special treat when we do manage to make that happen.

Mostly, we just enjoy being together.

We generally try to avoid doing anything too competitive, since Jay and I are both fierce competitors. It has to be said that he usually beats me at whatever we do—especially tennis. I get so mad for losing—and since he loves to tease, it usually ruins our date night so we try to stay away from competitive sports or games to preserve the kind, loving nature of the evening together.

Getting our much-needed time away helps each of us to enjoy coming back together again. Distance doesn't mean we don't love one another. It's a healthy break, especially under circumstances such as ours. As we strive to keep our relationships with each other close and free of unresolved conflict, we find that our impact to the world around us is greater.

CHALLENGE #7
Unified Families Reflect God's Perfect Relationship with Himself

»» »» »» »» »» »» »» »» »» »» »» »» »» »» »» »» »» »» »» »

God lives in perfect relationship with Himself. It's a mystery that's difficult to understand, but God in the form of the Father, Son, and Holy Spirit lives together in absolute unity. This relationship is commonly referred to as the Trinity. Throughout the gospels, Jesus continually explains that He and His Father are one.

Unified families reflect God's perfect relationship with Himself. When a family loves each other and serves together, they reflect God's light to the people around them. They are like a bonfire to a world in need. Just as a fire draws you to its warmth and causes you to be mesmerized by its flame, so does the unified family that serves together.

Let's face it, maintaining family unity and loving those closest to you takes a lot of work.

» Will you strive for unity in your family?
» Will you love your family and be a conduit to reflect God's light?

We challenge you to serve together as a family and see how God uses your lives to shine like a huge bonfire to the world around you.

19 CRAZY LOVE

DECEMBER 14, 2008

We were set to leave Santa Rosa early in the morning. The RV was packed, and we had said our good-byes. The Matthews family was up early and gathered together to see us off. Instead of the usual roar of our diesel engine, all we heard was a rapid *click-click-click*. When we discovered the RV wouldn't start, our hearts sank. Jim Matthews made a couple of phone calls to a towing company he knew in town and was able to borrow two big battery jumpers. Before long, the engine was started and we were on our way to meet up with John and Jill Turner, friends from Atlanta. The Turners were renting a house in Camarillo, California, with a full RV hookup, including water, sewer, and electric right in their driveway. John offered to let us come there for as long as we needed to stay.

A couple of days after we arrived, LV Hanson, a friend of John Turner's, invited us to attend an informational breakfast meeting for Catalyst West Coast, a next-generation church leaders' conference. We were familiar with the Catalyst organization from their meetings in Atlanta. This meeting was taking place in Simi Valley at the Reagan Presidential Library. We heard that Francis Chan, the author of *Crazy Love*, was going to be speaking at this event. Several of our friends had heard him speak and were deeply moved by his message of radical love.

We knew his book had taken off and was doing really well and we were eager to hear what he had to say.

Francis Chan passionately spoke about his three-month sabbatical where he began asking all sorts of questions about his life and his faith. During those months, he sat down to read the New Testament cover to cover and discovered the revolutionary teachings of Jesus in a fresh, new way. He explained that his church had a $60 million building campaign in the works and how he realized that as the lead pastor he couldn't bring himself to approve that project. He questioned what his church was doing—and how they were really helping the world. He didn't see how the excess of this building matched up with the teaching in the Scripture he preached. He suggested they keep their old building and erect an outdoor amphitheater. He thought they ought to give away the rest of the money they had left over to feed the hungry and clothe the poor. The church went for his idea, giving the excess money to overseas missionaries and orphanages and other worthy causes. We were moved by his story and could easily see why people were embracing the *Crazy Love* message.

At the end of his presentation, Francis Chan challenged the pastors and people at the meeting to get back to the Bible and the ways of the early church.

Our eyes were filled with tears, and our spirits sounded a resounding *YES!* Our hearts became knitted to the message Francis Chan shared with us on that morning we first heard him speak, and we realized there was an obvious symmetry between his church and our mission.

A couple of weeks later we decided to visit Cornerstone Community Church in Simi Valley, where Francis Chan was speaking. We thought it made sense to attend one of his services to see if we felt the same way we did when we saw him at the Catalyst breakfast. He gave a powerful message on purity that day. Hearing him speak again, we realized that he was extremely authentic, had the humility and passion for the Word of God, and spoke straight from his heart. After the service, we waited around hoping we'd get the chance to meet him. We shook his hand

and quickly told him how inspired we were by his message. It was a brief meeting that left us wanting to know more about what was in his book that everyone was talking about.

We picked up a copy of *Crazy Love* to read so we could familiarize ourselves with the full message of the book and not just the bits and pieces we had picked up along the way. It sat on the nightstand for a couple of weeks without either of us cracking it open, which was kind of odd because we were genuinely interested in reading it. Time seemed to pass by so quickly, especially with the holidays upon us. It didn't seem like we had a moment to breathe, let alone read.

20 A VACATION FROM OUR VACATION

When traveling in an RV, sometimes other people can think you are on vacation all the time even though the reality is that you have to keep working, schooling the kids, and keeping up with life. We had spent eight months traveling in the RV and felt it was time to take a vacation from our "vacation." We thought it might be fun to drive over to Utah to spend Christmas with Jen Hoglin, a friend we met in the summer of 2008 from Sprout Marketing, the firm that represents The American Academy. When we were in Salt Lake touring schools for Ben, Jen and her husband invited us to join them in Park City anytime. We decided to visit them for the week after Christmas to have some fun playing in the snow. We all agreed that we would forgo Christmas gifts and instead would take a family vacation to Utah.

We have always dreamed of taking our children on a family ski vacation, but the expense of that type of trip had generally made our dream out of reach. The Hoglins' generous invitation was the first time we could experience such a trip because they were allowing us to stay with them for free.

We spent Christmas Day in Camarillo, California, parked at the Turners'. They lent us a makeshift tree that was made out of a tomato cage. Ben, our resident creative genius, made nineteen ornaments to hang on the tree, each representing the states we'd visited over the past eight months. The other kids strung popcorn together, made skiers out of pinecones, and the three wise men out of peanuts. This was one of the most special and memorable Loecken family Christmases we can recall. It was simple, yet intimate.

On Christmas Day we downsized the contents of the RV and fit everything we needed for our ski trip into our Honda Pilot before hitting the road for the twelve-hour drive to Utah. About halfway into the drive, we swore we'd never pile into that car and take a road trip again. Whatever complaints we had about traveling in the RV would no longer be considered valid or worthy because that was downright luxurious compared to all of us being squished into the six-passenger SUV with our snow gear in tow.

The Hoglins' home was beautiful. It overlooked the snow-capped, majestic mountains where we would spend the next several days playing in the snow. The family let us take over their entire basement, which was fully furnished, including a full kitchen and bathroom. It was a perfect setup for us. We didn't want to be totally intrusive on the Hoglins—after all, it is a lot to invite a family as large as ours into your home for a week.

Much to our surprise, through some of Jen's connections at Sprout Marketing, we received a phone call from Krista Perry, the Marketing Director for Park City Resorts. After hearing about the ARK Tour, she called to offer us two free days of skiing, a full-day ski lesson for all of the kids, and one day of tubing on the mountain. We were completely blown away.

By January 1, 2009, we made our way back to California. After we returned, the biggest and most immediate task that had to be handled was the rebuilding of our website, which turned out to be a frustrating and painful process. Not only did we have to reconstruct everything, but we also lost all of the blog entries and comments that people had made over the course of the nine months we'd been on the road. That loss saddened us as we had nothing tangible left to reflect upon, only our memories.

Note to self: next time you want to transfer your entire computer over to another computer, make sure you talk to a real "Mac Genius" and not someone behind the counter who thinks he is a genius. We learned that lesson the hard way!

We ended up spending a total of five weeks parked at the Turners' in Camarillo, California. During that time, we enjoyed sharing meals and having great conversations with John and Jill. We also kept busy with school, service projects, and a few day trips.

We are always sensitive to the fact that when people invite us to park at their home, we never want to overstay our welcome. People have shown us amazing hospitality along the way, and we hope that we never take advantage of their kindness.

Whenever we hook up in someone's driveway, there is always this beautiful exchange of give and take. They offer us water and electricity and the use of their home and laundry room; and we, in turn, provide meals, babysitting, organizational help, cleaning, a listening ear, or whatever else would be of service to their family.

In the end, we walk away with peace knowing we not only were provided for, but that we met real needs of theirs as well.

We finally said our good-byes to the Turners on January 17. We drove for most of the day to reach Irvine, California, the next stop on our journey. With no place to park in the area, we did what we often do in that situation—we reached out to some local churches to see if we could park in their empty lot.

Our friend LV Hanson had office space at Mariners Church. Mariners is a nondenominational, multi-location, megachurch located in Irvine, California. Thankfully, LV was able to help us arrange to park in their lot. Finding a church that will agree to let us park is no easy task. For the most part, they will offer a night, maybe two. Their theory is that if they let us park there, they'll have to let their entire congregation or anyone else with an RV park there too. We had much better luck with small rural churches than we did with big city ones, which tend to be more political.

Much to our delight, the facility's manager agreed to let us stay. This was good news because our generator had stopped working and needed to be serviced. It was much easier to get the work done in a more metropolitan location.

㉑ DO SOMETHING!

JANUARY 2009

JAY» I was sitting in the RV still working on our website when I heard a car engine outside that wouldn't start. I could tell from the sound that the battery didn't have the gusto to turn over the engine. I grabbed my set of jumper cables and walked over to the broken-down car. When I approached the vehicle, I could see that the guy inside was obviously frustrated. He was gently knocking his head against the steering wheel.

At some point in our lives, we've all been there, right?

I knocked on the window, being careful not to scare him, and asked if he needed a jump.

He tried starting the car one last time before saying, "Sure."

As I placed the cables on his battery, I handed him one of our cards. I explained who we are and briefly told him what we were doing. After I got the car started, I encouraged him to pay this act of random kindness forward. I walked away thankful that I could give the guy a helping hand.

A couple of hours later, I received an e-mail from the stranger I helped that night. He wrote:

> *I am the gentleman you helped out in the Mariners parking*
> *lot. I want to thank you for helping me. I was having a rough*

*night, and you totally changed my mood. I feel that God sent you
to help me out as an angel. I feel totally blessed that you helped
me in my time of sadness. I am still in shock about all of this
because I didn't expect to meet you.*

All I did that night was give his car battery a jump. It was a simple
act that took less than ten minutes of my time. You never really know
what is going on in someone's life, which means that even the smallest
act of random kindness can make a big difference. There were obviously some much bigger issues going on with the guy I helped that night
that God knew about. But I surely had no idea what those were when
I knocked on his window.

Acts of random kindness are sometimes spontaneous and other
times well-executed plans. It doesn't matter which way they come as
long as you *do something*—anything. Choosing to do nothing is the only
way you can be certain you will never have a moment like the one I
shared that night. Have the courage to step out in your faith, trust your
gut, follow your instinct, and take action. You never know whose life
you may change, but you will always be clear that yours will never be
the same.

While we were in Irvine, we decided to visit the Crystal Cathedral,
located in Garden Grove, a short drive from Irvine. On the particular
day we attended services at the Crystal Cathedral, Francis Chan happened to be speaking. You can probably imagine how surprised we were
when we found out that he was the guest speaker. We silently wondered
why our paths kept crossing. We listened to him speak powerfully about
eternity and what each of us is truly living for. He asked a very good
question that got us thinking: "Are you living for this life, or are you
living for the next?"

We were really moved by Francis's message—even more than the
first two times we heard him speak. After the service, we browsed
around looking at the different buildings and checking out the gift shop
before heading to our car to leave.

Just as we were pulling out of the church parking lot, Francis and his wife were leaving the church and walked directly past our car. I rolled down my window, leaned out of the SUV, and said, "It's funny how we keep running into each other," and then handed him my card. Somehow, a message was being sent to me, if only I would listen to it. So finally, it seemed like a good time to pick up Francis's book and give it a read.

The very next day, my cell phone rang. It was a number I didn't recognize at first. When I picked up the call, it was Steve Hooper, a guy I had interviewed with for a job as a sales manager six years prior. He owns a clothing and merchandising company that sells to thousands of churches across the country. The job didn't pan out because Steve wanted me to stay in Orlando, where we were living at the time. We were planning on moving up to Atlanta, so I had to pass on the offer. Even though I didn't take the job, Steve and I had kept in touch and talked a couple of times throughout the years. In fact, I had e-mailed him back in October 2008, just as the bottom of the mortgage business was falling out, to see if he had any possible part-time job opportunities. I heard he had gone on a sabbatical, so I wasn't terribly surprised I didn't hear anything back from him until this particular day.

We made the usual small talk for a few minutes. He told me that during his sabbatical he began to read the New Testament and was praying for sometimes up to six hours a day. God had really touched his heart and now had a tight grip on it. And then he launched into the real reason he was calling.

"I recently read a book called *Crazy Love* that has transformed and changed my life," Steve said. "It has rocked my world, Jay. Have you read it?"

My jaw just about hit the floor. I was a little shocked by the nature of his call but very interested to hear where he was headed. I told him about the interactions we'd recently had with Francis Chan over the past several weeks and how I had just started reading *Crazy Love*. We were both amazed at the timing.

He explained that after reading *Crazy Love*, he phoned Francis Chan to say that he believed God was calling him to get his book into the hands of every youth pastor in the country. Intrigued, Francis shared with Steve that he and his elders at his church had just been praying that God would bring them someone who could help promote the message in *Crazy Love* in ways they weren't able to.

Steve had done a lot of work with churches, ministries, and youth groups in the past, making T-shirts for them and donating a lot of his services for free. He had a huge database of people, and he could market products to anyone. He came up with a campaign that he called The Whole Revolution. It was designed around random acts of kindness and paying it forward though a medallion that the person doing the act of service would hand to the recipient. I thought it sounded like a really great idea, although I wasn't sure why he was telling me all of this.

"Jay, I want you and your family to lead the way for this movement. You're already on the road, which makes you perfect to head up this campaign where you go out and mobilize people. Your prayers have been answered, Jay. I want to pay your salary to have you and your family keep doing what you're doing. My company will take 1 percent of our gross sales, which is around $75,000 a year, and give that to you as a salary. All you need to do is get the message behind *Crazy Love* out there."

Like most deals that come along as this one did, Beth and I took time to talk it over. We thought that maybe God had brought Steve Hooper to us. I hadn't read the entire book yet, so I decided to finish the book and pray about it before I made my final decision. We seemed like the perfect fit for this since we were already on the road trying to mobilize others to serve. Logically, I was having a difficult time coming up with valid reasons to turn him down, so I agreed. I figured we could give teeth to the message Francis Chan was stirring in people. Also, there was a growing *Crazy Love* movement happening. Why wouldn't we join forces to become more effective as one than we would ever be as two apart?

Steve is a visionary who gets an idea for something and then figures out how to turn that idea into a reality. We were intrigued to say the least, but something felt off from the start. Still, we continued our conversations almost daily, where we'd sometimes talk for hours about all that God seemed to be doing and about the mission that we felt called to accomplish. As we continued our conversations, we decided the best way to move forward together to accomplish our objective was to start a nonprofit 501(c)(3) ministry called Crazy Love in Action.

While we were both convinced that God was leading us in this direction, we knew that God was going to have to show Francis this as well so we could use the name that was synonymous with his book.

We were able to arrange a conference call with Francis and his agent so Steve and I could share our story and our vision with him. Thankfully, he too felt God was moving. The last hurdle we needed to get over in order for us to move forward was to get the approval from the publisher of *Crazy Love,* David C. Cook, based out of Colorado Springs.

From the very beginning of this association, Francis Chan chose to stay at arm's length from us. He is a man who likes to keep a low profile, doesn't want a lot of attention, and didn't want it to appear that he had hired us to promote his book. He is the furthest thing from being a self-promoter. He's simply passionate about God's truth and desires to wake up the church of America. He didn't want anyone to have the perception that he was using us to sell his book for profit—his or ours. He wanted everything to grow in an organic way—which meant he didn't want to have anything to do with the planning but was willing to allow us to move forward using the name.

To us, Francis Chan is the real deal. He lives out everything he writes and speaks about. He donates all of the proceeds from his book to a foundation he set up, which then gives the money to various worthy causes to benefit the poor and needy. He continues to live as a true inspiration to us in every way.

Things were getting off to a great start, although we still had to get his publisher on board. Steve and I flew out to Colorado to present our idea. We thought the meeting went well, although they said they'd be in touch with their final answer.

While I was waiting out the response from the publisher, I continued to be concerned that our family needed to have an income. I was reluctant to let go of my work in the mortgage business until I knew that everything was a total go from Steve. I was nervous about our partnership from the beginning; but I held onto the belief that God was ultimately in control, so I accepted what Steve said while things were coming together.

In the meantime, I was still in need of some repairs on the RV and was desperate to find the cheapest way to get them done.

Throughout our journey, God has woven an amazing web of relationships into our lives. While we have met many great people along the way, there are those who really stand out who have helped champion our cause.

One afternoon, I was inside Mariners Church sketching off their Wi-Fi while we were still parked in their lot. I was in the midst of trying to coordinate getting our generator fixed at a place in Oceanside, about sixty miles south of where we were parked.

Beth was at the RV and was getting ready to leave with the kids for the afternoon when she heard a knock on the door.

When she opened the door there was a man there who said, "Hi. My name is Dwight Hansen. I saw you and Jay speak at New Vintage Church in Santa Rosa around Thanksgiving. I have relatives up there that took me to their church on the day you were there. I walked away from that service really inspired by what you shared. Where are you headed to next?" he asked

Even though Beth didn't recognize the man at the door, she felt it was safe to speak with him. She explained that we were temporarily staying at Mariners Church. As soon as the details were worked out, we were planning to head south to get our generator worked on.

"What kind of engine do you have in the RV?" he asked.

Beth wasn't sure, so she quickly gave me a call on my cell. I told her we have a Cummins engine.

When she told this to Dwight, he said, "I work for Cummins! Let me see what I can do."

I wasn't sure how much it was going to cost to fix our generator, but I knew it was going to be expensive and, without a doubt, more than we had budgeted for the repair.

The very next day, Dwight called to say we could take the RV over to the local Cummins shop where they agreed to fix our generator and change the oil for free. That was a $700 savings for us!

Once again, God was working His ways to provide for and take care of us. Dwight was so thoughtful to hook us up with the incredible people at Cummins, but that wasn't all he did.

A few days after we arrived at Mariners Church, we were informed that we'd have to leave the church parking lot later that night. Dwight immediately offered to let us park in front of his home. And as if he hadn't already done so much for us, Dwight called over to Newport Dunes, an upscale RV park in the wealthy beach community of Newport Beach—about twenty minutes west from where we were parked—and made arrangements for us to stay there three nights absolutely free. That particular RV park charges upwards of ninety dollars a night, so that too was a significant savings for us and a wonderful, unexpected, and much-appreciated gift.

Dwight quickly became a good friend to us. He took our family boating, invited us to his home to watch the Super Bowl, and went above and beyond what we could have ever imagined from someone we had just met.

Dwight asked where we were headed to when we left Newport Beach. I told him we were heading south to San Diego. He said that Cummins had a motor home branch there they had recently shut down because of the economy. He was certain they still had active hookups right on the premises that we could use while we were in the area. Once again, he made a phone call to make sure it would be possible. Sure enough, we would be able to stay there with free hookups for our entire stay. Dwight explained that Cummins has a foundation that gives to worthy causes. When they heard about us, they wanted to do whatever they could to support us in what we were doing.

There are simply no words to express our gratitude for all of the kind generosity Dwight and his family and friends showed us. He had no ulterior motive in providing the several opportunities he opened up while we were in the area other than to simply help us out. We have marveled at how all of these things came together at just the right time—and at Dwight and his unbelievable service to us. People like Dwight have taught us about what it means to proactively think of needs and meet them without ever being asked. We have seen how God watches over us through people that He puts in our path at the right time and the right moment—even if it appears to be out of the blue.

Sometimes life on the road can be lonely, scary, and uncertain. Stepping out into the unknown on a regular basis has challenged our faith and caused us to see what our hope is in. It is no longer in money, nor in living in safety and luxury—it is in God and God alone. Even though we continually feel like we are free-falling off a steep cliff, God has shown up in human form through Dwight and many others to remind us that we are not alone and that He's got our back.

It felt like getting the approval from Francis Chan's publisher took forever, but by February 2009, we had come to an agreement where we could use their logo with the understanding that they could pull back that right at any time, for any reason. They didn't want to take the risk on us tarnishing their brand, which we completely understood. They did give us a couple of cases of books to give away on the road; but other than that, they made no other commitment beyond the use of the logo.

We were so excited to be a part of this new and amazing adventure and couldn't wait to spread the Crazy Love in Action message.

Several months earlier, we were contacted via e-mail by Margot Gilman, deputy editor of *Ladies' Home Journal*, who said she had been following our story through our website for several months and was intrigued. She contacted us to see if we'd be interested in having their magazine do a feature on us.

We had started to receive many calls and e-mails from people who wanted to profile us in their local papers or do a news story on us—and even one asking us to appear on the television show *Wife Swap,* which we turned down.

We actually gave the idea of doing their television show some thought until we realized that the show is based on extremes and melodrama. We didn't want to compromise our message or exploit our family for the $20,000 they were offering to appear on their show. Considering our financial situation at the time, it was tempting; but we knew in the end that it wouldn't be worth it. We didn't want to ruin everything we'd been working toward for fifteen minutes of fame.

When *Ladies' Home Journal* called, they seemed genuinely interested in the work we were doing. We both had conversations with the editor to make sure the direction of the article meshed with our message and purpose.

Several months passed after they made their initial contact. Neither of us thought they were going to go through with the interview. It may have been that they were keeping an eye on our progress that kept them at bay for so long or perhaps they simply lost interest. We didn't give it much thought until one day they reached out again. This time they wanted to send a writer and photographer to meet with us.

We were planning to serve at the Orange County Rescue Mission when they came to do the interview. They shadowed us for the day as we served lunch and ice cream and played games with the kids. They told us the article would run in August 2009. That was the last we heard about the piece for some time, which was fine since our plates were now fuller than ever.

STORIES OF THE OBSESSED

JANUARY 25, 2009

BETH» When we started this trip, I could never have imagined that I would leave little pieces of my heart all over the country. I feel strangely happy and sad all at the same time about the relationships we have formed over the past nine months. I can hardly put into words the depth of impact meeting so many memorable people has left on my heart, especially those families where the parents are coming off of some type of addiction, choosing to clean up their lives and making tough choices to create better opportunities for themselves and their children.

We saw a glimpse of these remarkable and beautiful families at the Orange County Rescue Mission. As we served lunch, we tried to fill each of the families with hope and encouragement, hugs and laughter. They seemed so happy to have our family there, especially when we rolled out dessert—ice cream—which we decided to provide as a surprise treat.

Ben, Bekah, Abigail, and Noah were at the helm as more than a dozen kids crowded around them and the five giant tubs of ice cream we brought into the cafeteria that day. With bowls and spoons in hand, they each picked their favorite flavor and topped it off with whipped cream.

One of the young boys asked Abigail what The ARK Tour meant on the front of her T-shirt.

Jay and I were interested to hear her answer.

"The Ark is the name of the RV my family lives in, and the tour just means we ride all over the country serving people."

The little boy didn't say another word—that is until he asked if he could have two scoops of vanilla.

Being at the Rescue Mission was a small token of our love, but to them it was hope.

Hope.

An inspirational word with so much power and significance.

When I listened to the stories from the people in the mission that day, I felt as though I could identify with their hurts and understand their struggles.

I was reminded of how each of us desires something deeper…something more out of life. These longings can be buried deep in our hearts or bubbling out of every pore. We all have goals and desires that seem to go beyond our reach. Maybe you daydream or fantasize about what could have been or what could be, yet continue to struggle with shortcomings, low self-esteem, or the belief that you can't, won't, shouldn't, or wouldn't make the necessary changes to achieve your goals.

I wake up each day with secret desires—I want more character, patience, kindness, and wisdom. I want more out of life, more time to do the things I can never seem to get to, and more desire to do the things I know I should do.

As I looked deep into the eyes of the women I met that day at the Orange County Rescue Mission, I made sure to tell each one how proud I was of her. These women are heroes because they are fighting hard to break out of their old ways to pursue a better life, free of addictions and entanglements. When you think about it, aren't we all trying to do that? You don't have to be addicted to drugs or alcohol to suffer from an addiction that holds you back. You can be addicted to shopping, money, food, sex, the opinions of others, or worry—just to name a few. From that perspective, maybe we are all addicts in one way or another. And though I've never thought of myself as an addict in the traditional sense, I am really no different than the people we served that day. As

I spoke to each of these women, I was keenly aware of our similarities and how we all have common threads in our lives even if we walk on different paths.

The power of serving comes from giving; but ultimately, you get so much more in return. For a few hours, I get to step out of my life of comfort and my tendency to focus on my own desires and allow God to show me my frailty and deep need for something so much greater than myself—Him.

JAY» Once we had the green light on Crazy Love in Action, it was as if the floodgates opened for us, with the first order of business getting the paperwork completed to start the process of filing with the IRS for the nonprofit status. We had to create a board of directors, and then we thought it made sense to get the RV wrapped with Crazy Love in Action all over it.

We began to head east toward Atlanta. Steve and I, along with our creative director, Jarod, had a meeting scheduled with Francis Chan in May.

One of our stops along the way was in Albuquerque, New Mexico. Once we got settled, I began looking for places to serve. I often looked up relevant churches in the communities we traveled as they are great resources in connecting us with individuals and nonprofits that are making a difference. I reached out to Matt Bradshaw, the Service Pastor for Sagebrush Community Church, one of the fastest growing churches in America. Matt and his wife invited us over for dinner; and after we shared our mission with them, he suggested that I call a radical guy named Gerald Martinez. Matt told me the Martinez family had been featured on ABC's *Extreme Makeover: Home Edition* a year earlier and they had quite a story. I was excited to meet with Gerald; at this point in our journey we had decided to do short videos on people who were doing radical things for those in need and post them on our website as a way to inspire others to do likewise. We would call the short video vignettes Stories of the Obsessed, something that was inspired by the *Crazy Love* book.

I liked Gerald from the second I met him. He was my kind of guy—he wore a T-shirt and a pair of jeans, had long hair, and sported a full beard accompanied by a sparkle in his eyes. He reminded me of Jerry Garcia. We spent several hours together swapping stories as I observed him interact with several of the men and women who lived with his family in their newly designed *Extreme Makeover* digs.

Gerald had been a successful sign maker. He and his family had a nice house in the foothills of the Sandia Mountains, and he was used to making around $500,000 a year. He and his wife, Liesa, felt called to move their family into what was known as the "war zone" of Albuquerque. At the time, this area was notorious for its extreme and violent crime. They experienced firsthand the prostitution, gunshots, and drug dealers. They saw it all, up close and personal. One time, Gerald was even chased down by guys with cinderblocks and was hit over the head with a glass beer bottle, ending up with a deep gash on his forehead.

In spite of the challenges they faced living in this area, they were committed to staying in the neighborhood no matter what obstacles were placed in their path. They have now called this neighborhood home for the past twelve years. Over that time, they've seen the crime rate come down by 50 percent. Gerald was and still is a driving force in helping to change the landscape and statistics of his neighborhood.

As we walked the streets, it was obvious that Gerald was not only the pastor of the local church, but also the "pastor" of the neighborhood. I was amazed at his relational skills as he interacted with his neighbors, as well as the many men and women who live on the streets in his neighborhood.

Gerald and Liesa have a heart for the hurting. There are young people who have come to their door looking for a place to stay and others who want to better their lives and get help to overcome addictions. Next to the Martinezes' home, they have a men's house and a women's house. They share their finances and food, and they live as a big family in community with one another. He is selective and careful as to whom he allows to live in the homes, as he wants to see that they want to better themselves and improve their lives and that they can be honest and live in community with others.

Gerald and I really enjoyed each other's company, and he and Liesa invited our whole family to have dinner with their family that evening. We took them up on their offer, and we had an incredible time and our families instantly meshed together. They invited us to park our RV next to their home and provided us with water and electrical hookups. We stayed with them for a week, and it was unforgettable. Gerald has this amazing ability to "do life" while including others in any way he can. Even a trip to Home Depot becomes a relational opportunity and not just a chore. Gerald and I often went on motorcycle rides and ran errands, and our families spent many late nights hanging out sharing stories. It was also fun to get to know the young people who lived with them. We even got to participate in a weekly drum circle that the young people from Joshua's Vineyard, their family church, did in the city. The experience is all about a way for this group to reach out to their community and connect with one another. It's not religious so much as it is a way to bond and build a bridge.

I learned so many things from Gerald, one of which is the importance of relationships. I tend to be extremely driven, and when there is business to do I get things done—sometimes at the expense of others. Gerald taught me a life lesson—not through his words but through his actions—that, at the end of the day, relationships are more important than business or getting a deal done. I had no idea how beneficial this lesson would become to me in the future. We left Albuquerque, sad to say good-bye but inspired for the journey ahead.

We headed toward Amarillo, Texas, and then on to Oklahoma City, where we wanted to see the sight of the infamous 1995 bombing. We didn't realize that we had arrived on the actual anniversary of the incident.

When we went to the site, we were told that Ann Curry, from NBC's *Today* and *Dateline* programs, was doing a question-and-answer session after a commemorative ceremony for the victims. After Ann spoke, Beth and the kids, along with many others, made their way to the front to meet her. She was warm and friendly and asked where we were from. When Beth told her what we were doing, she was so inspired that she yelled out to the entire room, "Hey, do you know what this family is doing?"

We were a little embarrassed by the unexpected shout out, but were touched by her sincerity and enthusiasm for what we were doing.

Shortly after Ann's introduction, a reporter for the local Fox affiliate approached us to say she'd like to do a story on our family. They came out to see us the next day and followed us around the city as we handed out homeless care packages and bought hot meals for some people we met along the way. The story aired on the news later that night.

At this point, we were still moving forward with Crazy Love in Action, so we felt that the story could be beneficial in helping to spread the *Crazy Love* message. It was uncomfortable for us to have cameras follow us as we worked with the homeless. We wanted to be careful to maintain their dignity. We also didn't want to give the impression that we were serving only for the camera. In the end, the story was extremely positive, and we hoped it would make an impact on viewers to go out into their communities and make a difference.

We left Oklahoma with our final stop being Atlanta. We were excited to be heading home—or at least to the place we had called home before embarking on our journey.

Finally, we had to redesign our website to incorporate our new name and association, again, with Steve's company agreeing to finance the lion's share of the expenses. Our plan was that by June 1, we would be working full time for Crazy Love in Action.

23 LIFE IS SHORT, ETERNITY IS LONG

Our new association with *Crazy Love* and reading the book ultimately challenged us to take a deep look at our lives and re-evaluate everything we were doing. It made us question whether our acts of service originated from hearts that are crazy in love with Jesus or if we were striving for the approval of others. Were we really living out what is commanded in the Scriptures? Was our family living with eternity in mind, or were we only living for this life? These were some really deep and heavy questions that were pecking away at us while softening our hearts all at the same time.

Francis Chan makes an analogy in his book of how we as Christians are swimming upstream against the current. If we stop swimming, we naturally drift downstream with the world and culture with which we live in. We both confessed to God that we wanted to fall more in love with Him. We wanted to make much of Him. We wanted to lead our children spiritually and be a tool that is useful in His hands.

We were reminded through *Crazy Love* that life on earth is short. We don't know when we will take our last breath. Francis talks about a friend of his who was asked if he was spending too much time serving or giving too much away. His response was, "I wonder if you will say that after we're dead."

We knew that everything that we did moving forward needed to be done in light of eternity. The why behind what we were doing had been answered and there was no looking back.

CHALLENGE #8
Life Is Short, Eternity Is Long

»» »» »» »» »» »» »» »» »» »» »» »» »» »» »» »» »» »» »»

There are only two things that will last for eternity: God and people. With that in mind, the only thing that matters in this life is how we love God and those who surround us. Nothing else will last.

Jim Elliot, a famous missionary who lost his life reaching out to the Auca Indians, said it well: "He is no fool who gives what he cannot keep to gain that which he cannot lose." Jim understood that the things in this life were temporal, but the things that he did for God were eternal and they would last forever. You can't take anything with you when you die. As the old joke goes, you'll never see a hearse pulling a U-Haul!

King Solomon, the wealthiest and wisest king who ever lived, came to the same conclusion. He had it all—wine, women, wisdom, and riches. He denied himself nothing he desired. "He refused his heart no pleasure" yet he concluded that "everything was meaningless and a chasing after the wind." Nothing was gained from his pursuits. He described this life as a "shadow that quickly passes away" (Ecclesiastes 2:10–11).

Several months back, we got a phone call from a close friend of ours explaining that his mother-in-law died unexpectedly on the operating table. The same day, we received news that a good friend of ours from Atlanta had tragically fallen five hundred feet to his death while climbing on Stone Mountain.

Life is short. None of us knows when our heart will stop beating.

Eternity is long. One day we will all stand before God. When you stand before Him, you won't be thinking about your 401(k) or your landscaped yard. The only things that will matter are your relationships and what you did for Him and others. Nothing else matters.

> » Will you live your life in such a way that you will have no regrets on the day you stand before God?
> » Will you live each day with eternity in mind?

We challenge you to love God with all your heart, mind, and strength and to love those around you as if today were the last day of your life.

24 DISCOVERING MY PASSION

ATLANTA, GEORGIA
MAY 2009

JAY» Being back in Atlanta was good for all of us as we visited with old friends and attended our former church. Our meeting with Francis and his agent went well. After talking with him, we all seemed to be on the same page. We were excited to see what would become of this new venture.

We spent the first week parked in our friends', the Waltons, cul-de-sac. Their small group from church was doing a book study on *Crazy Love*. They asked us to come and share our story with them and discuss some of the topics Francis Chan addresses in his book. We had a great time, and we really connected with the Waltons' neighbor and friend, David. The book had caused him to reflect on his life and question if he was giving all that he was able to by leveraging his resources to follow the vision God was giving him.

David and I connected right away. I loved his passion for people, and it was obvious to me that something was stirring in him from the core of who he was. Since we were parked right next to his house, it was easy for David and me to hang out. Having just spent time with Gerald Martinez, I took a page out of his book. Over the course of the next week, we spent a lot of time together getting to know each other. It was as if we'd been friends our entire lives. It was clear to both of us that our meeting wasn't an accident.

Our connection with *Crazy Love* brought us to another milestone in our journey when we realized that it wasn't just enough to inspire people to serve; but in order for lives to change, we needed to inspire them to action. With this new enlightenment we decided to invite the Waltons, along with their neighbor David and his wife, and several of their other friends, to come with us to serve under the bridges in downtown Atlanta. At first Randy Walton wasn't crazy about the idea. Although he had volunteered hours of his time and served in leadership roles in a number of nonprofits in Atlanta, going under the bridges was way out of his comfort zone, and he was concerned for the safety of his wife and daughters. But his wife, Crista, was excited to go. She has a huge heart for people in need, and she wanted to break out of her suburban bubble to see firsthand what was happening only thirty minutes from where she lived.

The following Saturday the Waltons, along with three other families, joined us under the bridges working alongside Seven Bridges to Recovery. It was an unforgettable day for me. I wept as I watched these families lovingly interact with the homeless. The highlight for me was watching a white suburban housewife walk hand in hand with an African-American woman who had made the decision that after three years of addiction, despair, and hopelessness, today was her day to come off of the streets. I'll never forget her words, "Today's my day! Today's my day! I'm comin' off the streets today!" That image and those words will be forever burned in my memory.

The events of that day had a significant impact on the Waltons. They were so inspired from serving that Randy began using his abilities as a consultant to serve inner-city ministries in Atlanta. Crista, a teacher, took her classroom under the bridges and they even wrote a book on their experiences. That day also had significance for me. That was the day that I better discovered my passion. That was the day that it clicked for me that I was doing something that uniquely fit who I am as a person; and what brought meaning, purpose, and joy to my life was seeing others come to life as they stepped out of their comfort zones, broke past their fear, and served others.

I recently took the StrengthsFinder 2.0 test by Gallup Organization, and my top five strengths are as follows:

#1 Activator

#2 Maximizer

#3 Communication

#4 Strategic

#5 Woo (Woo stands for winning others over)

The role I've found myself in is a complete hand-in-glove fit. I'm a deeply passionate person who loves to activate and mobilize others to serve those in need. It excites me to find people's strengths and to help them nurture, refine, and stretch their abilities toward excellence. Our journey as a family was also a journey of personal self-discovery for me. I was seeking to identify a role to which I could give myself that had significance and at the same time leveraged my unique personality, life experiences, skills, abilities, talents, and passions. I was able to use my strengths to inspire others to join us in significant work that was not only impacting those we were serving but also those who served.

This was the day that I discovered that my unique role and calling was to activate and mobilize people to act on their faith. I was to help people leverage their strengths and empower them to serve others with their talents. I was to use my ability to communicate to win and challenge others to serve those in need. This was something that came effortlessly to me and I knew it was something I could give myself to for the rest of my life.

As if this wasn't enough, something else happened that day that I will never forget—something that would help sustain us for months to come. As David and I served together under the bridges, he began to ask me questions about Crazy Love in Action and our financial needs.

The day before we went under the bridges, I had a difficult discussion with Steve where he explained how much money it was going to take to build our new website, wrap the RV, and do the Whole Revolution campaign. Since the costs had come in higher than anticipated, he told me that he didn't think I'd be able to start working full time in June unless something financially big happened for us. The problem was that I had been turning away mortgage deals with the promise of beginning full time in June under Crazy Love in Action. When David began inquiring about our financial needs, I was hesitant to respond as I didn't want him to think that I had an agenda for our friendship. He pressed me for an answer, so I told him that we needed roughly $30,000 for the initiatives we had planned so that I could begin working full time on June 1.

He looked at me and said, "Done."

"What?" I asked.

He said, "Done," and then explained to me that he had just sold his BMW for $30,000. He said he wanted to donate the money to Crazy Love in Action.

Of course I was shocked, overwhelmed, and moved to tears all at the same time. I was floored by David's generosity and how this amazing gift came at just the right time. We kept moving full-speed ahead with a fresh spring in our step, and the next order of business was getting the RV wrapped in Crazy Love in Action.

Getting the RV wrapped is not as easy as it sounds. We wanted to make sure the design was exactly what we wanted. We decided to work with a web-based company from California who had an installer in Atlanta who gave us the best price. It took a couple of weeks; but before we left Atlanta, the job was done. It was good for everyone because our RV became a tremendous marketing tool for the Crazy Love brand.

By the end of May, we left Atlanta for Nashville, Tennessee. We were excited to launch the newly wrapped Crazy Love in Action RV. On the drive up, we noticed a lot of people stopping and staring at the bus. Our plan was to drive directly to Steve's office at Uth Stuph (pronounced *youth stuff*) so he and his employees could see the RV. When we arrived in the parking lot someone came up to us and asked if Francis Chan was on the bus. A couple other people questioned us as to what we were doing.

As we were making our way into the Uth Stuph offices that day, unbeknownst to us, a man walked in behind us with a certified letter for Steve. The letter turned out to be paperwork for a lawsuit that his business partner had filed against him. It turned out there were multiple reasons for the lawsuit, one of which was Steve's partner's disapproval of the funds committed toward us and Crazy Love in Action. The situation got ugly…and fast. Without knowing it, we were now at the center of their firestorm. Because of the pending lawsuit, Steve was unable to make good on the financial promise he had made to me. This was one of my worst fears coming true.

This was an extremely difficult time for Steve, as he was not only watching his business decline but was also losing his business partner and lifelong friend. We tried to move forward with all the initiatives we had planned, but all of Steve's time and emotions were focused on the financial and legal problems that he was now suddenly facing. We both also came to realize that we were the kind of guys who like to be in charge. We were both great visionaries with different approaches toward reaching the same goal.

I realized that if your collective vision is off, even a tiny bit, you will never hit your target. We both concluded the partnership was not going to work and parted ways as gentlemen. We decided to continue using the name Crazy Love in Action for what we were doing as a family, since we now had a bus wrapped in the name and we believed in the cause.

When I look back on everything that happened, I now realize that the only business partner I will ever have again in my life is my wife.

There is a bright side to this story, though. I had the idea to start a nonprofit rolling around in my head for months when Steve initially reached out to us. I knew there was a lot of red tape and hoop jumping that goes into starting a nonprofit. Had it not been for the *Crazy Love* experience, I am not certain I would have had the courage, stamina, or drive to take that dream and turn it into a reality all on my own. It certainly wouldn't have happened as quickly as it did once we aligned ourselves with *Crazy Love*. So if I am being completely fair about the experience, I would say that there were definitely some good things that came out of that association, despite the break up.

We had to refocus and regroup…again. We realized we had to go back and reconnect our initial goals, what we were out on the road doing and what God was calling us to do. We couldn't make it about anyone else's dream, agenda, or plan—even if it was a worthy one. No, we had to get back to center, come full circle, and revisit what our intentions and purposes were when we left Atlanta and the mission we had set out to fulfill.

We didn't want our work to be about us. We were seeking to create a movement that God was stirring in us so that we could stir it within other people.

We did not want to compromise our core beliefs, values, and goals. I wanted people to know what we believe, even if it hurt us in the end. We are unashamedly Christian without pushing too hard at anybody. If that makes someone not want to be a part of what we're doing, then that is his or her choice. We will never force someone to see things our way because it isn't about us—it's about God and His ways.

We are not afraid to speak what we believe. We are not going to deny our faith or beliefs just because they may make some people uncomfortable. This is who we are and what we do. We aren't trying to push our beliefs on anyone, but we do want to show and share with others that having a relationship with Jesus is the most incredible experience we've ever known. We are not here to *save* anyone. We have no power to do anything but lead through example. God is the only one who wields that power, and our goal isn't to shove that down anyone's throat. Our only goal is to love other people and share our journey. If they're searching, we've got answers from the Word of God that we're more than happy to share. Our message isn't about a particular religious belief or church affiliation—it's for all people, Christian and non-Christian alike.

25 LADIES' HOME JOURNAL

JULY 10, 2009
INDIANAPOLIS, INDIANA

The article in *Ladies' Home Journal* finally hit the newsstands in July 2009. Since the interview took place five months earlier, we were eager to see the article when it came out.

We weren't prepared for the unexpected onslaught of e-mails we received as a result of the article. People were reaching out to us with all sorts of offers and invitations. We were also peppered with hundreds of e-mails filled with words of encouragement, which meant the world to us. People wrote to invite us to speak and share at their churches, offered free hookups for the RV, told us about service opportunities in their areas, and so much more.

We were genuinely excited by the interest people showed. The article was the first major national exposure we'd had. We had ticked ten thousand miles or so when we did the interview. Five months later, when the article came out, we had doubled that number; and we're still counting. Everything we were working toward was coming closer into sight. We were truly grateful for the article and the opportunity it provided to give glory to God.

We weren't certain about how this was going to unfold, but we did our best to stay close to God and simply continued to join Him in what He was doing before us every single day.

We left Indianapolis on July 25, 2009, and headed north toward Michigan. There have been several times on our journey when we questioned what we were doing and wondered if we were actually making an impact on people. Whenever those moments of doubt and insecurity seeped in, something wonderful happened that would remind us that everything we've done has been worthwhile.

Shortly after the *Ladies' Home Journal* article came out, Jim Horn— pastor of the Clio Church of God near Flint, Michigan—contacted us. He was hopeful we'd be able to come to Michigan to speak at his church. The timing was perfect as we had been thinking of heading north to see Troy and Jennifer Schrock, the couple we met and stayed with in Breckenridge, Colorado. They lived in the Detroit area, about an hour south of Clio. We let Pastor Jim know we'd be happy to come up his way and share with his church.

We stopped in Detroit for a couple of days where we spent the bulk of our time visiting with Troy, Jennifer, and their family. It was wonderful to reconnect and see some familiar faces. We also invited them to serve at the Detroit Rescue Mission with us. We had seen how inviting people to serve with us inspired them to want to serve too. We toured several of the Rescue Mission facilities, most of which were at their capacity. After seeing our options, we decided to serve at the women's and children's shelter.

Marci Fitch, Director of Volunteer Services, showed us around and hosted our family throughout the day. Marci came from the film industry, where she had spent much of her time with celebrities. She told us about meeting Clint Eastwood when he was in Detroit to film *Gran Torino*. While working on the movie, Marci helped the Detroit Rescue Mission launch a health clinic. During her time as a volunteer, she realized that working with those in need was a much more fulfilling role for her, so she decided to stay on and continue working with them full time. Marci and her dedication to those in need blew us away. She told us that although it was cool to hang out with celebrities, it didn't compare to the blessings she found working with the Rescue Mission.

After our time in Detroit, we headed north to Clio, where Bud and Val Worthing—one of the families from Jim's church—offered to host us. They let us hook up the RV to their home during our stay. They had full fifty-amp power, water, and sewer right on their property. For RVers, it doesn't get much better than that. We were looking forward to seeing what God had in store for us—as, once again, we felt it wasn't a coincidence that Pastor Jim had reached out to us.

After sixteen months on the road, our journey became many things to us. First, it has been about serving God and His glory. He called us to go out and demonstrate our faith by serving others, and we stepped out and obeyed Him as best as we knew how.

Second, it has been about the heroes of the faith who feed the hungry and care for the widows and orphans day in and day out without any recognition.

Third, it has been about mobilizing ordinary, average people to get out of their comfort zones to discover their unique gifts and then use what God has given them to bless others.

When we hear a young boy say he likes serving, as he helps an elderly woman get to her car with a bag of groceries, it makes it all worthwhile. When you see the sparkle in the eyes of a woman from the suburbs making friends with a woman from an inner-city shelter, it makes it all worthwhile.

When a fire is ignited in a pastor and he challenges his congregation to mobilize, step out of their comfort zones, and serve, it makes it all worthwhile. These things all began to happen in Clio, Michigan. Pastor Jim was one of those pastors who grabbed on to an opportunity to inspire his congregation.

We came to Clio unaware that we would find a group of people who were tired of living the status quo. They desired to reach out and show the love of Christ that was inside each of them.

Sometimes all we need is someone to come along and ignite the fuse to help us see that there is more to life than the daily grind that can mindlessly box us in.

When we got to Clio, Pastor Jim greeted us by taking our whole family on a grand tour of the area. His one condition was that we do the tour in our RV. He was excited to be in the RV as we drove all over town, including to Frankenmuth, the number-one tourist attraction and destination in Michigan. Frankenmuth is considered Michigan's "Little Bavaria." The village looks like it was plucked from a hilltop in the Alps and gently placed in the middle of Michigan. We even toured the famous Bronner's Christmas Store, but just the sight of Christmas ornaments in July brought back horrific memories of Jay's former job working in a similar store in Chicago. He made a beeline for the door, fearing he might be subjected to some rendition of Mannheim Steamroller!

JAY» Our hosts, Bud and Val, were truly amazing people. Bud, a seasoned RVer, helped me fix several things around our RV that had been broken far too long. Unfortunately, Bud became a little more intimate with us than he probably expected or desired.

That night, Bud offered to let us dump our waste into his sewer located in his driveway. There must have been a kink in the hose, causing pressure to build up in the sewer line. We both heard a small explosion where the main sewer line attaches to the RV. When we realized what happened, we were in shock as waste and toilet paper flew all over Bud's lawn.

I stood frozen, watching in horror and unsure of how to stop the flow. It was like everything was happening in slow motion. That's when I heard Bud yell, "Close the valve!"

I reluctantly reached my hand in to shut the valve, but not without suddenly becoming covered in brown debris. After the whole embarrassing ordeal had ended, Beth felt bad for Bud, saying "Poor Bud."

Looking back, I was the one covered in poo. Maybe she should have felt bad for me too! Thankfully, Bud and his wife just laughed it off before handing me a bottle of bleach to clean up the mess.

After settling in to our new temporary home, we realized our time in

Clio was going to be a bigger experience than we had expected or planned on. God usually likes to change our plans because His are always much better. The trick is to give up control and let God do His thing.

A couple of days after we arrived, a reporter from the local ABC affiliate came to do an interview with our family for the evening news. They had selected us as their "Persons of the Week." We also did an interview with the Frankenmuth *News*, and a radio interview with 106.9 FM, "The Light," out of Asheville, North Carolina, which has a listening audience of 400,000 people or more. We really enjoyed talking with Jerry Woods, the afternoon drive-time host. Requests for interviews with our family seemed to be growing, especially since the magazine article came out. Suddenly, people knew who we were, which was odd to get used to. It's always an honor to be asked; but we were never terribly comfortable doing these types of interviews, as we didn't want the focus to be on us, but rather on inspiring others to live in action. To accomplish this, we always tried to keep the focus on serving and direct it away from us as a family.

While we were in the area, someone who had been following our blog connected us with Dick Rottiers, who runs Flint Outreach Center located in the heart of Flint, Michigan—one of the most depressed and broken cities we had seen throughout our travels. Dick is truly living out the commands in Scripture. His ministry is feeding ten to twelve thousand people a month. After meeting us, he invited us to come and share our story with the members of his church.

When we spoke, twenty-five people from Clio Church of God came down to help serve the hungry with us after the message. In less than two hours, we served food to more than 140 people. That was by far the largest number of people we had seen at one facility in that short period of time.

It occurred to us, after sharing with Pastor Jim's church, that it wasn't enough to talk to people and give an inspirational message. We had to actively take steps to get them to join with the projects we were doing. Pastor Jim was instrumental in getting us to see that the cycle worked best by sharing our story and then inviting people to come with us.

As our three weeks in Michigan came to a close, we were reminded of how gracious our heavenly Father is. He has provided so many wonderful opportunities for us during our journey, but especially during our stay in Clio. We made a lot of new friends, shared fellowship, and laughed. We also received brand-new carpeting for the RV thanks to Hal and Kelly Earegood and Jim Dourst. We were even treated to free dental cleanings, thanks to Dr. Sam Salem Family Dentistry, who was kind enough to offer cleanings for the whole family.

Seeing the dentist was a regular thing for our family back in Atlanta. All it required was a simple phone call to our family dentist, but life on the road has changed that ease and convenience. Even though we still had insurance, it cost us several hundreds of dollars in co-payments every time we went. We'd only had one other check-up and cleaning since we hit the road back in Santa Rosa thanks to a generous woman named Grace Colbert, so we gladly accepted this dentist's gracious offer. We were grateful for his kindness. It felt great to have clean teeth and to know that our dental concerns and a few small cavities were taken care of.

We experienced people putting their faith in action during our stay in Michigan. It was refreshing and inspiring. God's greatest work is in the hearts of men and women. We have experienced love, depth, and encouragement that we simply cannot put into words in those believers we have met along the way. As we reflect on the time we've shared with others on the road, we are reminded that the only thing that will matter for eternity will be what we did for Christ. In that moment, when we stand before Him, all of our efforts will have been worthwhile. God's continual guidance in our ministry brings us daily comfort because we know, without a doubt, that God orchestrates all things, so therefore, He deserves all of the glory.

26 WIPED OUT

AUGUST 17, 2009

There have been many times during our journey where we have been just plain old wiped out. When we left Michigan, we were all really tired and ready for some downtime.

Beth had to start preparing for the start of another school year, while Jay was working hard on the video elements for our website. Although we are rarely apart, it also felt like we needed some real bonding time together as a family too. We looked for a place where we could unwind and get away from it all, but the location also had to be on the way to our next stop. We were heading to Saratoga Springs, New York, because we received an e-mail from Mike and Janice Reeves asking us to come speak at their church, New Life Fellowship.

Shortly after we left Michigan, we received a call from Nola and Mark Auernhamer, a family who lived in the Niagara Falls area who had read about our family in the Frankenmuth newspaper while visiting relatives in Michigan. They were hoping we were headed toward New York in our travels and would consider stopping in their area when we did.

Although we had never been to the area, we were certain a few days in Niagara Falls was exactly what the doctor ordered. The Auernhamers connected us with the folks at the Niagara Falls Bible Conference, who allowed us to spend a week at their camp, which overlooked beautiful Lake Ontario. The sunsets over the water were spectacular. On a clear day, we could see Toronto across the lake. The camp had a miniature golf course, a little village made for kids, a swimming pool, and a fire pit; and best of all, Niagara Falls was a short drive away. We were able to explore the falls, which were beautiful and breathtaking. Our week at the camp was filled with lots of family fun, rest, and catching up. We also had the opportunity to briefly share at the camp's Sunday evening church service with members of local area churches in attendance.

We arrived in beautiful and historic Saratoga Springs on August 28, 2009, just in time to serve with Mike and Janice at the Backstretch Ministry at the Saratoga Racetrack, the oldest thoroughbred track in the United States.

The Saratoga Racetrack opened in 1863 and has been the perfect image of summer, wealth, and glamour. But for those who work behind the scenes, their jobs are anything but glamorous. Their days often start at 4:30 a.m., with a seven-day workweek. The pay is low, the work is grueling, and they live at the poverty level at best. The track workers are offered housing with no kitchens and must use a community bathroom. The racetrack is open for only six weeks during the summer, but the backstretch workers live near the area from April through October before moving on to another racetrack.

Most of the workers on the backstretch are poor immigrants and are often there without their families. We joined several people from Covenant Church who organize a weekly dinner and movie night for the immigrant workers. We were in awe of these loving people who saw a need right before them and met it. The next day we had a chance to tour the backstretch area. Our eyes were opened to a world we knew nothing about.

That Sunday we had the opportunity to share our story with members from the New Life Fellowship after their pastor gave an inspiring message entitled "What's in Your Bag?" based on the passage in John 6 where Jesus feeds five thousand people. Talk about perfect timing! The pastor's message fit together with ours like a hand in a glove. We knew that it was God's plan for us to be there on that specific weekend to hear that particular sermon.

By the time we got to Saratoga Springs, the children had all started school again. Ben was taking biology and needed a microscope for his lab assignments, but we didn't have the funds to purchase one. Jay's plan was to take Ben to the local high school of whatever area we were in to borrow one of theirs whenever his lesson called for it.

Unbeknownst to us, Mike Reeves is a biology teacher! When he heard about our need for a microscope, he was able to get a used one from the school where he worked and gave it to Ben. We were thrilled that Ben's school requirements for lab would be met right in our RV and without having to make treks to find the nearest high school. Mike continued to serve our family by helping us collect odd materials that we needed for future science projects and experiments. He also guided us to check out helpful websites with lots of useful information for reference.

We were very fortunate to get to know the Reeves family. They let us park in their driveway and were very hospitable to our family. They let the kids ride their horses, jump on their trampoline, and relax on their hammock. At the end of our time we all enjoyed a huge bonfire together.

BETH» A few weeks after we left Saratoga Springs, I received a phone call saying my dad had fallen ill again. This time my family said I should come back to Kansas City as soon as I could, as they didn't believe he had long to live. I quickly made the arrangements to fly that same day out of Portland, Maine, the nearest metropolitan airport to where we were parked.

My dad had some touch-and-go moments for the week that I was home. While I hated to leave him, it appeared he was on the mend, so I made a reservation to fly back to Maine to re-connect with Jay and the kids. I vowed to call my father every day so he'd know I was thinking of him. While it was difficult for me to not be by his side, I knew I was where God wanted me—home with my family and back out on the road doing what we, as a family, felt called to do.

27 GOOD MORNING AMERICA

So much of the time we had spent on the road felt like an exercise in patience. We were chugging along, slowly chipping away at defining our purpose and then putting that vision into action. Still, we couldn't shake our feelings of waiting for something big to happen or wondering if we were supposed to be doing something different with Crazy Love in Action. Francis Chan and his publisher had been so gracious to us, but now it was time to step out on our own so we could pursue our original vision.

JAY» Truth be told, the waiting was a challenge for us in two ways. First, I am not a terribly patient man, especially when it comes to business. I like things to happen lickety-split. When things don't go down that way, I can—and usually do—become frustrated.

Second, our money was almost gone. We needed to get a break soon or we'd be completely out of cash. We were down to living solely off of whatever was left from our savings. Money was flowing out and there was nothing coming in. I thought about going back to work selling products to mortgage companies—at the very least part-time, so I could bring in some additional cash until things came together. When I left the company, they told me the door would always be open for me if I ever wanted my old job back. When I reached out to talk to them again, the metaphoric door had been sealed shut. Though I was disappointed, I accepted that it wasn't meant to be.

I looked at some other opportunities that were nothing more than cash flow, but all of those seemed to fall through too. It got to the point where it appeared that I was supposed to move forward with Crazy Love in Action full time and continue to pursue our nonprofit status, which needed some reorganization if we were going to move forward.

Perhaps the craziest and most exciting development from the *Ladies' Home Journal* article was receiving a call from a producer for the ABC morning show, *Good Morning America*, saying they'd like to feature our family on their "AmeriCAN" segment. These segments focus on people who, seemingly against all odds, are making a difference in the world. Chris Cuomo, who has since left the show to anchor *20/20*, hosted the segments. Chris is a very funny and down-to-earth guy.

Maureen, the producer of the segment, spent several days getting to know all of us. She was so much fun to be with that she became an extended member of our family. They taped the segment in New York City on October 19, 2009, but it didn't air until October 30. In between the taping and the airdate, we decided to head to the nearby Pocono Mountains.

Maureen asked us to come back to appear live on the show after the segment aired. She wanted us to drive the RV through the very busy and crowded streets of New York City, which was quite an undertaking. While we had gotten much more proficient at navigating the RV through cities since our disaster in New Orleans, we have to be completely candid and say that driving in Manhattan was daunting, and intimidating.

The staff at *Good Morning America* was able to secure a safe parking spot for the RV in the heart of Times Square for the night. They arranged for all of us to check into a hotel next to their studio. We had to be up and at it by six o'clock in the morning the following day to be camera-ready for the show. We couldn't arrive in Times Square until after midnight, so by the time we parked, checked into the hotel, and our heads finally hit our pillows, we only got three or four hours of sleep. We have the utmost respect for the entire team at all of the morning shows, as we now understand what a grind it can be working those crazy hours!

We felt amazingly thankful to have the opportunity to appear on the show, especially because roughly five million viewers would be exposed to our message and we could continue to give God the glory. If just one viewer was somehow touched enough to make a change, volunteer their time, give their gift to another, then it would be worth every moment leading up to this appearance. We knew we had the chance of a lifetime in front of us. We had no idea what would happen next.

While we were in New York City, we met with Brian Johansson, the vice president of the Bowery Mission. We were filmed serving at one of their locations in the city for the *Good Morning America* piece.

Before we left the mission, Brian asked if he could talk with us. We didn't know what was on his mind but were eager to find out.

"Can I be honest with you?" Those words hardly ever end with something good, but in this case, they would. "I'm really confused about what you do. What's your mission? Why do you have *Crazy Love* across the RV?

Whoa.

Brian's questions were fair and well pointed. We gave him the only answer we had.

"We're still trying to clarify that, Brian."

His candor was refreshing and totally real. He came at us with such vigor, which we totally appreciated. He told us he was surprised we had lasted as long as we had on the road because we didn't have a real champion behind us. We were not being supported and sent out, nor was anyone financially helping us along the way. It was God and us. Brian said we were like "missionaries without the support of a church."

We knew Brian had years of experience and wisdom in this area, so we spent hours talking with him, picking his brain about what his thoughts and ideas were. He shared his mission statement and vision for the Bowery Mission, which gave us a solid business model to base our next moves upon.

We left that meeting with one point perfectly clear. We had a lot of hard work ahead of us; but this time, we would have a solid plan in place before we moved forward any further.

Our first order of business would be to take the final steps to separate our movement from the *Crazy Love* association. We knew we wanted to come up with a different name for our organization that totally re-branded us. This time we wanted it to be something that would immediately be associated with us and not some other group. We wanted to take our time to think about the right name, because this time would be the last time.

The confusion being Crazy Love in Action brought was that people thought we either wrote the book, worked for Francis or his church, or that reading *Crazy Love* is what caused us to sell our home and go on the road. All in all, it was confusing; and it was best for us to step out of it and go back to doing what we felt called to do as a family.

Every experience we've had brings us closer in focus, creating a clearer picture of our mission and goal. Our association with *Crazy Love* was a tremendous learning and growing experience for us.

From the moment the *Good Morning America* segment aired, our life became a rapid blur. It felt like everything was moving in fast motion. Within hours of the show, we had more than two thousand hits on our website, more than one hundred e-mails, dozens of requests to come speak at churches all over the country, and a possible book deal.

Moments after the segment aired, we received an e-mail from twelve-time *New York Times* bestselling author Laura Morton.

Okay, we have to be totally honest. We had never heard of her. But we certainly knew about several of the books she had written. She e-mailed us to see if we would be interested in possibly writing a book. You can probably guess the end to this story, but we are going to tell it to you anyway.

We weren't sure what to make of Laura's e-mail and the subsequent phone calls that followed. She certainly had the credentials to write a great book for us, but we had no idea how the process worked.

Laura explained that she had lunch with an editor from a publishing house she knew well a few weeks earlier who said she was looking to acquire books that not only inspire people but inspire them to action. She was very clear on the parameters of what the book could and could not include. After seeing our feature on *Good Morning America,* Laura instinctively knew we'd be the perfect fit. All she had to do was get the publisher on board, which she believed she could do and it would be a go.

We've heard stories about how hard it is to get a publishing deal. People suggested we self-publish our story because publishers wouldn't go for something like this. It wasn't mainstream enough. We didn't have a platform. No one knew who we were. And so many other reasons writing a book about our journey would never happen.

All of this would have been accurate and true except for one thing: God's plan was to have us write a book—this book.

We were totally overwhelmed by the pace that this new opportunity was happening in. After careful consideration, we called Laura to tell her we wanted to take thirty days to make any decision so we would have time to pray and seek wise counsel. She agreed that there was no hurry and that we ought to take whatever time we needed to make sure this was what we were supposed to do. And to help our process along, she offered to introduce us to her literary agent at William Morris Endeavor, the largest talent agency in the business.

We drove from Pennsylvania back to New York for a face-to-face meeting with Mel Berger. We sat in his very impressive office staring at hundreds of books he keeps in his office of authors he represents, ranging from Bill Cosby to Nancy Pelosi. We couldn't help asking ourselves what we were doing there.

Mel understood us and what we were looking to do right away. He recognized what we wanted to do with our book and how he could help make all of that happen. He seemed like an honest and decent man who had an appreciation for what we were trying to accomplish.

Still, we wanted to take it all in and move cautiously and with purpose. We never thought we'd be weighing our options to write a book or do a reality television show when we first started out on this adventure. But here we were—suddenly faced with making the right decisions for the right reasons. We had to take money out of the equation, even if we were more financially strapped than ever. We had to listen to what God wanted us to do and base our decisions on His plan.

Throughout this process, we were reminded by God that what He values and what our culture values are not the same.

He values the simplest things.

He cares about our relationships with each other and our children.

He cares that we keep our priorities in order. His concern is for the poor and needy.

That is where His heart lives!

We took the full thirty days to weigh all of our options. After talking to Ivo Fischer, television super-agent and all-around great guy, we decided that doing a reality show was not an option for us. Even though it would be tremendous exposure, it didn't feel like a fit for our family. We didn't want to give up control of our message. We felt that it would become too intrusive. We weren't willing to give up editorial control where someone else would have the ability to alter our message.

Writing a book, however, made perfect sense. We were thrilled with the opportunity given to us by Linda Cunningham, our editor, who got on board right away. It was Linda who gave us the final push to officially change the name of our ministry. We spent a couple of weeks writing out our strategy, mission, and core values. We took the documents that Brian had given us and came up with what would ultimately become our new mission—to inspire, empower, and mobilize people to put their faith in action.

BETH» Now that we were more focused, we were excited to move forward and begin to implement our plan. Several weeks earlier we were contacted by Donn and Cyndie Truax, who had seen the article in *Ladies' Home Journal*. They invited us to come and share with the youth group at their church where Donn was one of the youth pastors. We rolled up to Matthews United Methodist Church in Charlotte, North Carolina, a congregation of roughly five thousand people. They generously let us park the RV in their church parking lot and provided us with water and electricity. We shared our story with the adult Sunday school classes and then were invited to a luncheon afterwards.

Because my dad's health had steadily been declining, I was on edge daily as I waited for updates. I had made trips to Kansas City each time we thought he was near the end, and then he would suddenly turn a corner and his health would improve. I was grateful for the time I spent with him, because we had deep conversations and special father-daughter moments that I would have otherwise missed out on.

As we finished our luncheon, I suddenly had this heaviness in my heart and felt an urge to check my phone for any messages. There was a missed call from my oldest sister, Theresa. The pit in my stomach grew. I knew there was a chance that my dad would pass and I would get the dreaded call, but my hope was that I would be able to get home to see him one last time.

I stepped out of the room to call my sister. She said my dad was unconscious and they thought he would go at any time. I was overwhelmed with emotion. I tried to go back to the table to finish my lunch and the conversations with the people at my table, but the tears suddenly burst forth and I explained my situation and excused myself from the luncheon. Under the circumstances, everyone understood my reasons for leaving.

Cyndie met me at the RV and made it her priority to get me on the next flight available. I'm not sure what I would have done without her. She contacted a friend who worked for the airlines who immediately booked the flight. I had to leave within the hour.

My mind was scattered. Thoughts raced through my head about the possibility of getting home too late. I wondered if my dad might possibly turn a corner—or if this was really it? Would I be able to say good-bye, and would he even know I was there? I also had concerns about the kids, their schooling, who would watch them if Jay had to fly home for the funeral, and what we would do about our commitments with Matthews United Methodist Church. We had service projects scheduled. Ben was set to speak that night to the church youth group. Still, I had to go.

I kissed everyone and dashed off to the airport, getting to my flight with little time to spare. Although my dad and I struggled with being close in my childhood, over the years we grew to have a deep and loving relationship that covered over all the pain from the past.

When I arrived in Kansas City, I was taken straight to my parents' house where my dad was lying in his hospital bed still unconscious, but alive! I kissed and hugged him multiple times and told him how much I loved him, but there was no response. I sobbed. My two sisters, step-mom, and I sat by his side. We talked to Dad as if he could hear every word—and I believed he could. Suddenly we saw his eyebrow twitch as if to say, "I know you're here, Beth." He seemed to be struggling to communicate with us as his hand started to twitch as well. I felt a flood of comfort come over me. My prayers were answered. I was able to say good-bye to my dear, sweet daddy who heard my every word. He was letting me know that he loved me. I felt it.

JAY» After Beth left for Kansas City, the kids and I prepared to go to the youth group that evening at the Methodist church. There were about five hundred young people, and the place was alive with excitement. I shared a brief message and then Ben talked about three life lessons he'd learned on the road. I was so proud to see Ben step out and do something that was out of his comfort zone. You could have heard a pin drop as the young people listened to someone their age, to whom they could relate. After he finished, he said he enjoyed it—and we don't think it hurt that he received twenty-three friend requests afterward on Facebook, with twenty of those requests coming from girls.

That evening I spoke to Beth and found out how her father was doing. We knew his time was coming quickly, so I began to look into a flight so that I could be by her side. I booked a flight for the next day, and then made arrangements for the kids for the next couple of days that we would be gone. I was thankful that it worked out for us to be together as I didn't want Beth to experience this alone. I knew she would have her family and that she would find strength in them, but I also wanted her to feel my love and support.

BETH» At 8:10 a.m. the next morning, twelve hours after I arrived home, my dad took his last breath. A wave of emotion shot through my body. I felt the intense sting from the reality of suddenly being orphaned, yet at the same time I felt such peace and hope knowing that one day I will see my parents again. Then there would only be peace, joy, and no pain or sorrow. My siblings, stepsisters, my stepbrothers, and my stepmom were all in the room.

It was beautiful and peaceful to have my dad right there, in his home, surrounded by all his family. The love we all had for this man was overwhelming. He had such a way about him that caused others to light up. People gravitated toward his friendly nature. He was a good man who saw the potential in others and strived to bring that out. He lived a hard life as he saw his wife take her life, and then his own son, my dear brother Jimmy, five years earlier tragically end his own life as well. He carried many sorrows, but his big blue eyes were filled with such gentleness and love. He said he hoped he would be alive at least five years after Jimmy died to be there for the rest of us and he was. How thankful we all were to experience a natural, beautiful death that wasn't tragic or unexpected. Dad had given us all a sense of stability and love in the midst of all the challenges in our life.

JAY» After the funeral, we all headed back to Charlotte and spent a very low-key Thanksgiving with the Truax family. Beth decided to stay back at the RV as she needed and wanted to spend time alone to process all the emotions she was feeling.

During our stay in Charlotte, we were racking our brains trying to think of an appropriate name for our new organization. I was obsessed with the task and often got up in the middle of the night brainstorming and writing down possible names. Every time I would come up with what we thought was a great name, I'd look it up on the web and would discover it was already taken by another group or the domain name wasn't available.

After weeks of what seemed to be an exercise in futility, the name finally came to me. Passion to Action—or P2A for short. The name was significant as it stood for God's passion and love that He has for us and then people identifying their passion and putting that into action to serve others. It was a perfect fit! And luckily, the domain name for the website was available too.

We were all excited to move forward with our new name and identity, but we knew the task that was before us with rebranding our whole identity was daunting. Still, I knew it had to be done.

28 WITH THE FAITH OF A MUSTARD SEED

DECEMBER 2009
CHARLOTTE, NORTH CAROLINA

JAY» When we do service projects, we encourage the people who host us to find people who are making a difference in their area that they can support. Cyndie Truax had heard about a woman near her home in Matthews, North Carolina, by the name of Joy McGuire who was serving those in need. I decided to meet with Joy before the service project so I could do a story on her for our website. As I drove onto her property, the first thing I noticed was row after row of vinyl tents. At first glance it looked like a flea market. As I walked around her property, I noticed that each tent was filled to its capacity with clothing, toys, books, and household goods.

Joy had lived a hard life and she wore it on her face. While years of addiction and difficulties had weathered her appearance, her spirit had not been crushed. Her eyes filled with tears as she described her former life of drug addiction, homelessness, and time in prison. She explained that her calling was to demonstrate the love of Jesus to people who are where she once was and to meet their physical needs. Her desire to give back began organically where Joy would receive clothing or household goods and then she would give it to someone she knew was in need. Because of her job as a social worker, she saw the needs for herself and was certain that those gifts were meeting real needs.

Things continued to grow over time to where she now has over forty tents on her property along with a metal shed to house all of the donated items given to her to distribute to others. We realized Joy needed help organizing and sorting through all of the donated items she had been given. She was overwhelmed and tired from managing her constant flow of inventory, not to mention the fact that she was caring for her bedridden husband. We made an appeal to the people of Matthews United Methodist; and the next Saturday, we had more than forty people show up to help Joy organize. It was powerful to see so many people come together to serve someone who had sacrificed so much to help those who needed it most.

The highlight of the day was when the whole group gathered around Joy, laid hands on her, and offered up a prayer for her and all that she was doing. Tears rolled down her face as we prayed. It was a powerful moment for Joy as she had received a much-needed influx of volunteers and support. It was an especially powerful moment for me as we saw that our strategy of sharing our story and inviting people to serve was effective in mobilizing people to action.

(29) DIGNITY SERVES

DECEMBER 20, 2009
MELBOURNE, FLORIDA

JAY» As 2009 came to a close, we realized we were going at a pace that was just too fast for us to keep up with. We didn't realize our own limitations and were constantly pushing ourselves beyond them, to our detriment. Pure exhaustion was setting in, which was taking a toll on everything from serving to our family life. We never felt as if we had done enough, as if we could have or should have done more for the people we were meeting along the way. We lost our balance a bit, which was impacting the sustainability of keeping up that breakneck pace.

We came to the realization that we only had so many hours in a day and limited dollars we could give to the process. We needed to become strategic about how we were going to spend that time. We needed to take some downtime to rethink our approach and to create a plan for how we wanted to spend our time moving forward. Also, the grief from Beth's loss was still rumbling under the surface as she had not had the time to fully deal with her emotions. She needed time to pull back, reflect, and rejuvenate. We knew that continuing to push forward would be harmful to all of us.

Beth and I spent hours working on a strategic plan based on our experience over the past twenty months of traveling. We decided that in order for us to make a difference in a community and to build relationships, we should stay in a city for two months at a time. Our plan was to share our story at a church, school, or event and then invite the people we spoke with to join us in a service project. We were adamant about not just inspiring people but mobilizing them into action. We also felt strongly that we needed a way to empower and train those that we mobilized.

I put together a PowerPoint presentation that visually told our story and explained our vision. Then I picked up the phone and started dialing for dollars. If someone had a heartbeat, I would show them my presentation over the Internet while I walked them through it via my cell phone.

While we were in Orlando, I reached out to my old friend Eddie Moratin, one of the most connected guys I know. I showed him my presentation, and he gave me some great feedback and suggested that I talk to a friend of his named Phil Hissom who was working in the Paramore District, a distressed community in the heart of Orlando.

When I met with Phil, he explained to me that he had written a curriculum on serving with dignity that was based on a community-development mindset. The study covered topics ranging from the importance of people to commitment. It talked about the concept of inviting the people that you serve to serve with you so that you don't create dependency, but rather raise a person's dignity. Phil shared his personal story of battling alcohol and how his life changed when he began to serve. He shared with me how he was working with seven homeless guys in Orlando; and that as a result of implementing the principles in the study and inviting the guys he was working with to serve with him, six of them had come off the street.

I wanted to experience the study for myself, so Beth, Ben, and I went through it in a weekend course that was offered. Next, we took the leaders' training and then signed up for another six-week class to really soak it all in. We began using this study in churches that we helped mobilize around the country. Eventually we came to realize that while this is an excellent study, it wasn't a perfect fit for our ministry. We began writing our own study, implementing many of the principles we learned from

Dignity Serves, as well as helping people identify their unique personalities, strengths, and spiritual gifts and how they can use the gifts God has given them to serve others.

While it was exciting to have our new Passion to Action name and strategy in place, we still had a ton of work to do. I decided to call Mark Morse, an old friend of mine who owns a cutting-edge advertising agency in Minneapolis. I needed help with a logo, marketing materials, business cards, a bus-wrap design, and a website. I figured it was a long shot, but I decided to call and ask him if his company ever did pro bono work.

When I spoke to him he said to me, "We do pro bono work for organizations that we believe in and people we like, and you fit both of those descriptions."

I was beside myself! I knew from past experience from my position as a communications manager at a nonprofit that design work is very expensive. The work that Mark agreed to do for us would range from $25,000 to $30,000 if we were paying customers. So many nonprofits have terrible marketing materials because they can't afford the money it takes to hire a professional. Thanks to Mark's generosity, we were able to dodge that bullet.

Another company that stepped up for us during this time was a T-shirt company in Orlando. I met the owner during one of the Dignity Serves classes that we attended during our stay in Orlando. We toured his shop, and we were impressed with the fact that they use only water-based ink, which is good for the environment. He loved our vision and he agreed to sell us T-shirts at cost, which took a little of the financial pressure off of us—every little bit helps.

Even though we took downtime during our four-month stay in Florida, God was always working. We were staying at the Lucky Clover Mobile Home and RV Park, in Melbourne, Florida, where we planned to spend the holidays. The manager was a rough-looking guy named Chuck. His head was completely shaved, he wore a long goatee, and he walked around the park with a parrot on his shoulder. As a kind gesture, Beth decided to bake Chuck and all the guys that worked at the park some homemade cookies. It wasn't much, but after seeing how hard they worked each day, she felt led to do it. That simple act wasn't a big deal, but it went miles with the guys. Chuck came by to say thank you.

"No one has ever done that for us," he said. "They mostly just give me a hard time." He was genuinely touched by that one single moment.

The simple act of giving cookies to Chuck allowed for us to get to know him better. When we went on walks and saw Chuck, we would stop and talk to him. One day, Chuck's wife mentioned that he wanted to speak with me. When I went into his home, he was sitting at the kitchen table with three beers in front of him, a cigarette in his hand, and his ever-present parrot on his right shoulder.

To be honest, I was a little intimidated by him. For whatever reason, Chuck always called me "Bo." I'm not sure why, but I got used to it and it didn't bother me.

"Tell me, Bo. Are you and your wife evangelists?" Chuck asked.

"No," I answered and then began to share our story. I didn't give him the long version—it was more the CliffsNotes approach, as I didn't want to overwhelm him with too much information. He appeared intrigued by what I had said and clearly wanted to know more about God. I could tell he wasn't completely comfortable talking because there were some other people in his house. I invited him to come down to the RV later if he wanted to talk in private. A few hours later, he came down. We welcomed him in and started talking and getting to know each other. It didn't take long for Chuck to open up and share some very personal information with me.

"You see, I've got a degenerative bone disease where my joints lock up. I haven't been able to eat solid food for two months, and I'm in an awful lot of pain. I was wondering if you could pray for me."

I had no idea Chuck had been battling a severe disease.

I told Chuck a little bit about my personal relationship with Jesus and how it has touched my life. "I'd be really honored to pray for you," I said. Before I prayed for Chuck, we had a lengthy discussion about spiritual things. He hung on every word and wanted to know more. I asked him if he would be interested in having his own personal relationship with Jesus too.

"Yes." That's all he said.

I didn't force that thought on him. Chuck is not the type of guy who would ever do something he wasn't completely comfortable with, so asking for this relationship was something he wanted all on his own. Beth and I invited him to open his heart and accept Jesus Christ as his Lord and Savior—and he did. It was a peaceful and inspiring moment for all three of us.

The next day, Chuck came by to see Beth and me.

"I don't know what you did, but I was able to eat for the first time in two months this morning. I got up and had a huge breakfast. I ate bacon, eggs, and all sorts of foods I haven't been able to eat for months!" He seemed to think we had something to do with his newfound appetite.

I explained to Chuck that we don't have magic powers and there was nothing we could have done that would have taken away the pain in his jaw and given him back his appetite. Of course, we all knew without speaking the words that it was something so much bigger than anything I said the day before.

God is big. It's not for us to judge or determine anything. All we can do is share what we know, love from our hearts, and offer peace and comfort to those in need. That's all we did for Chuck that day.

It was incredible for us to experience how showing a simple act of kindness and demonstrating God's love to Chuck in a tangible way paved the way for a relationship. That relationship then paved the way for Chuck to open his heart to God.

BETH» During our stay in Florida, I spent time weeding out and reorganizing the RV—something I have to do all too often. Things can easily get piled up, misplaced, and disheveled, causing us to do an overhaul. Each of us sorts through our belongings to see what can go and how we can better organize things for space and functionality. I have to admit, I love organization. Some women collect shoes, others handbags. Me?

I collect storage containers! It's become something of an obsession, especially since we moved into the RV, where every inch of available space must be used to its fullest capacity. The more organized I am, the more space I can create for all of us.

Even though the temptation for impulse buying is always there, my practical side usually takes over because we really do not have any additional space. I'm sure I could squeeze a few things in here and there; but I don't like clutter, and having more than I need is really unnecessary.

I now realize how I used to spend frivolously on things I truly didn't *need*. We have saved hundreds of dollars just by cutting back in superfluous spending. Of course, I didn't realize it was excessive until we learned that we could easily live without. Living simply is not about depriving yourself. It's about reducing the clutter and eliminating the unnecessary things in your life so that your time is more manageable and free to spend on other things.

I had to learn to turn off the constant bombarding messages we see daily on the road that shout, "More is better." I have discovered that I can live life more fully and freely without all of that extra stuff. When we have less to care for, our life is less cluttered and therefore our minds are less cluttered. We are then freed up to spend more time on our relationships and developing new friendships with other people we meet along the way.

Since we were all on board with the changes that needed to be made to accommodate living with even less, collectively cutting back was never a real issue for any of us—even the kids.

How did we accomplish this?

It was everyone's dream to make the adjustments so we could reap the benefits and rewards that are a daily part of our journey. We all realized there was going to be some give and take. For everything we've given up, we've gained so much more, especially when it comes to seeing and experiencing our amazing country the way we do.

WHAT IS IT LIKE LIVING IN THE RV FOR YOU?

»» »» »» »» »» »» »» »» »» »» »» »» »» »» »» »» »» »» »»

»» BEN

Overall living in the RV is pretty crazy! We are surprisingly able to all fit in the "enormous" 340-square-foot space comfortably enough during school. Everyone has his or her place (my place happens to be in the passenger chair with a TV table). During busy times such as lunchtime or Sunday morning, everyone is stepping on each other's toes, bumping into each other, or someone is constantly in someone else's way. However, living in the RV is a great experience and I really enjoy it!

»» BEKAH

Living in an RV is a once-in-a-lifetime experience. I enjoy living in an RV very much. Sometimes it is hard because we are all together all the time and you can't just go to your room and be alone. When we get in arguments, we have to work it out right away. I love living in an RV because history comes alive when we go sightseeing. We also get to help many people in need. Sometimes I miss the comfort of a home— to sit in front of the fireplace and read—but when I feel that way, I have to remind myself that God is my comfort and all I need is Him to be satisfied. Stuff never gives you satisfaction.

»» ABIGAIL

I love living in an RV, but there are some things that I am not so crazy about too. The things I love are that we get to see SO many places that ordinary kids with ordinary lives wouldn't get to see. Sometimes I don't even realize how blessed I am! I also love having friends all over the country that I can keep in touch with. There's just one problem, I have to be the "new kid" every time we go to a new church! It's mostly easy to fit in, but sometimes I just want to be around people that I have known for a really long time or I'm really close with.

»» NOAH

I like living in the RV. I like traveling around the country—it's really fun. I like being close to my family. Sometimes I wish I had my own bedroom.

One of the greatest advantages of being on the road has been taking something off the pages the children are studying for school and experiencing it for themselves. There is only so much we can learn from a book. When they get to see things close up, they never forget it.

A great example of this was when we ended up spending an entire week at the Toutle River RV Park near Mount St. Helens, the most active volcano in the Cascade Mountain Range. Seeing this remarkable and breathtaking horseshoe-shaped crater was an unbelievable experience for all of us. The children could see the volcano as they studied the cataclysmic eruption and the effect it had on the environment and the people in the region, and the science of what caused the explosion on the morning of May 17, 1980.

This type of involvement and participation is the greatest proof we can offer when people ask us what it's like to homeschool our kids. There is simply no substitute for the value they get in experiencing these various lessons while standing on sacred land, staring at Mount Rushmore, reading the actual Constitution, or visiting Ground Zero. A classroom environment simply can't compare to the vast lands we've covered zigzagging from coast to coast.

WHAT IS IT LIKE BEING HOMESCHOOLED?

»» »»

BEN »»» It's awesome! I actually really enjoy being homeschooled. I love being able to have my own schedule and not live in the stressed environment of public school (and I never have to worry if I'll get a bad a teacher).

BEKAH »»» Being homeschooled is so fun for me because we get to have our mom as a teacher. I love being able to stay home with my family all day, and we get all of our schoolwork done during the day so we don't have to do homework at night! Sometimes I would like to be able to go to school and have a regular life, but living in an RV is so much more rewarding.

ABIGAIL »»» There are pros and cons about being homeschooled. I'd say that the pros are getting to be around my family ALL the time! Another thing is that we get all our required work done in only four days of school! (BONUS!!!!) The cons would have to be...wow, let's see, there aren't that many. Well, the only one that I can think of is that we don't get to be around friends every day like most kids. Who really cares, though, if you've got your family?

NOAH »»» It's really fun. I really like my teacher. My favorite subjects are math and spelling.

30 WE ALL LIVE GOD'S STORY

When we first made the decision to take our family on the road, we realized that was based on our desire to put our passion into action. We recognize that most of you will not sell your home as we did. There's an old saying that one person's dream is another person's nightmare. The good news is you don't have to take such extreme measures to tap into your passion.

Regardless of who you are, or what religious background you have, we all have the privilege to live God's story. We came to this realization during our mission trip to Africa.

What was that trip really all about?

For us, it was coming to an understanding that God is huge—He lives everywhere.

God isn't being narcissistic by telling us what to do for His benefit; He does it because it is in our best interest. If we can learn to be quiet before God and let go of our own agendas, we would be much happier and more content on the whole.

A lot of people make the common mistake of believing the story is about them, so they live their lives in that selfish way. We too have been guilty of this. There is much more joy and satisfaction in giving yourself away and living for the sake of others.

Serving God is the greatest honor and the reason we made our life-altering decision. The love God has for us is endless. If you can accept His love and pursue Him with open arms, then His love will pour out from your life onto others.

CHALLENGE #9
We All Live God's Story

» »

If we've learned anything over the past several years, it's that the story is all about God. It's about His glory, and everything points to Him. The crazy thing is that He chooses to write us into His story. He's the central figure and the main character. We simply play a supporting role in His story.

Regardless of who you are, God wants to speak to you. You don't have to be a scholar or a saint to hear His voice. You simply need to be still. He will speak to you. He's concerned about your life, and He wants to use it to do something significant for Him.

Oftentimes we run around trying to figure out our lives while the answer to our concerns is right in front of us. We make the mistake of thinking that our significance comes from doing, while God's definition of significance comes from being. Before we can do anything of value for God, we need to learn to be with Him for our service to have power.

» What new role or script is God planning for you?
» Will you spend some time in prayer and accept His role and script for your life?

We challenge you to know your lines in your role by quieting yourself, being still, and listening for His voice.

31 PASSION TO ACTION

MARCH 30, 2010
ORLANDO, FLORIDA

JAY» As our time in Florida was winding down, we were grateful for the time of rest and margin to build a new foundation for our work. We received a call from a church in Minnesota that requested we come for June and July to help mobilize their congregation. We were excited for this opportunity, but we had a gap in our schedule for the month of May. Out of the blue, Beth received an e-mail from Jen Wiegers from West Lafayette, Indiana. She had read the article in *Ladies' Home Journal* while she was getting her hair done and was touched by what she read. She later went to our website and saw that we were in Florida and knew that she and her family would be visiting Orlando in the next couple of weeks. She is a Creative Memories consultant and wanted to stop by the RV and drop off a CD so we had a way to organize and display all the pictures from our journey.

Since the article first ran, we had been contacted by a host of different people, most of whom were very kind and sincere. There were occasional odd requests, which sometimes made us feel uncomfortable. E-mails and other correspondence is one thing, but a request for a face-to-face meeting was often something we were a little leery of.

When Jen first contacted us, we weren't sure how to respond. But something about her request felt right, so we took our time to consider it. We were trying to keep a simple schedule on our sabbatical, which meant we were being especially particular about how and with whom we spent our time.

After giving it some thought, we decided to meet with Jen and her husband, Brian, along with their four children. We really enjoyed our time together. Brian seemed extremely interested in our mission to mobilize people to put their faith in action. We agreed to meet in the morning for breakfast where I explained our strategic plan in more detail. He told me he wanted to share what we were doing with his church in West Lafayette. I didn't have high hopes that his church would allow us to come for the month of May since it was only a few weeks away. Brian and I spoke several times on the phone over the course of the next couple of weeks. I was shocked when he called to say his church was extending an invitation for us to come for the whole month.

We immediately began calling campgrounds in the area to inquire if they had availability for five weeks. We kept striking out—everywhere we called was booked. In the eleventh hour, Brian came through; he was able to connect us with a client of his named Jerry Brand who allowed us to park in the Taj Mahal of RV storage garages. He had a shed large enough to hold three forty-five-foot RVs along with full electric and water hookups and an attached two-car garage. For us this was like staying at the Ritz Carlton.

We were able to keep the RV out of the elements and have room to spread out. Our time in West Lafayette was nothing short of amazing. We were able to implement our new plan and strategy and help empower their congregation through teaching the curriculum on serving with dignity. We shared our story and invited people to join us in reaching out to a distressed local apartment complex we found out about through the church's post-prison ministry. Inmates who are released from prison often have a difficult time finding a place to live. This particular apartment complex welcomed all of the ex-cons regardless of the severity of their crimes.

We decided to go door to door to identify what needs the residents had as well as to find out what skills and abilities they had so we could work together to improve their community. We were floored to see more than 120 people show up on the Saturday of Memorial Day weekend to help landscape, paint, install screen doors, and reach out to the residents of Schuyler Avenue Apartments.

Several principles we were incorporating in our approach to service were implemented in this project. Before we got started, we went door to door asking powerful questions of the residents such as, "What do people say you are good at?" We were able to identify what skills the residents we were going to serve had as well as what the real needs were in their community. Once we knew what the needs were, we then invited the residents to use their unique abilities to help serve alongside of us. Our project included painting every door and all the gutters in the entire complex. We also painted and installed twenty screen doors and re-landscaped the front of the building. It was incredible to see people from the church working alongside of ex-cons. When one of the residents pointed out to us that a neighbor was handicapped and needed a handrail installed in front of his unit, we were happy to make sure he got what he needed. Having the residents participate in this project gave us the insight to help someone with a real need.

It was powerful to see the principles in the studies we were teaching being implemented and the effect that it was having on everyone involved. We knew that serving brought us joy. We had seen how it impacted people who had means and lived in the suburbs, and now we were able to see how serving brought fulfillment and joy to someone living in a distressed community. People were mobilized; and at the same time, we were able to identify needs along with the skills and abilities of the people we served. We invited those served to serve with us—and they did. A church was mobilized and ignited—and the icing on the cake was that they made a long-term commitment to continue to serve the residents of Schuyler Avenue Apartments on an ongoing basis. We drove away from our time there standing in awe of how God moved and were thrilled that our newly implemented strategy was effectively igniting people's passion and mobilizing them into action.

It was invigorating to move forward with a plan; but by this point in our journey, we knew that even the best-laid plans need to be held loosely.

We realized this when we arrived in Minneapolis to work with a church on the west side of town. In addition to teaching our weekly class on service, we taught an elective class on Sunday mornings for six weeks as part of their Sunday school. Since we hadn't done this before, it took a lot of work and preparation to teach the lesson each week.

By the third week of the Sunday school class, I knew I had to change things up a bit. I was getting stuck in the box of being the talking head at the front of the class. While I believe knowledge is important, if we don't act on that knowledge it's pretty much worthless. I knew from my past experience in sales that you learn more when you get your teeth kicked in from a client or when you make a mistake that takes money out of your pocket. You learn more from doing. Based on this experience, I decided to give the class a twenty-dollar challenge.

I asked for five people to give me twenty dollars. People jumped to their feet and I ended up with nine people who gave me twenty bucks for a total of $180. I then asked for nine volunteers. That wasn't difficult as they assumed they would receive some quick cash. Now that they were at the front of class, I explained the parameters of the challenge. They would have to agree to four things:

They couldn't keep the money.

They had to pray and ask God to show them where He was working and use that money to bless someone else during the next week.

They couldn't just give the money away; they had to leverage it by buying something or doing something creative with the funds.

They had to agree to be at class the next week and share about their experiences.

During the week I received a phone call from Dayna Murray, a successful real-estate agent and a participant of the challenge. She explained to me that as she prayed, she believed that God had placed the number four hundred in her head. She was led to take her twenty-dollar bill and turn it into four hundred dollars. She explained that she sent out an e-mail to her sphere of influence, roughly 230 people, to include them in the challenge and invite them to participate. She sent me a text message a few days later explaining she was well on her way to the four-hundred mark. She was now trying to figure out what to do with the money. I texted her back and told her that God knew what to do with it and to pray and ask Him to surprise her. When we spoke again she told me she whispered the prayer "Surprise me, God" immediately after my text while she was waiting in her car to show a house to a client. Dayna explained that she rarely brings her phone into a house she is showing; and if she does, she turns it off so she can focus completely on the home and her client. She was surprised when her phone rang. She decided to answer it since her client hadn't arrived yet. It was Beth Moorhead from Wayzata Free Church, whose responsibilities include handling requests for spiritual and financial assistance. Beth had caught wind of how Dayna was leveraging her twenty dollars and was calling to inform her of a need. Dayna told her how she had just prayed and asked God to surprise her. Beth said, "Surprise!" and explained how she had just received a call from a woman who was recently diagnosed with cancer. She couldn't make her mortgage payment because her chemotherapy treatments were making her sick, leaving her unable to work. Both Beth and Dayna were surprised and amazed at God's timing when they realized that the mortgage payment and the amount that Dayna had raised at this point were the same, $400.

The next week at class Dayna was one of the first people to share her story. She concluded with an update that her $400 had doubled to $800. Her money had doubled because more people from her sphere of influence decided to give and get involved in her cause. It's amazing how quickly and how big something can grow when it's planted from the tiniest seedling.

She explained how she was able to give the full amount to the woman with cancer as she had other needs in addition to her mortgage payment. As I sat and listened to Dayna, I couldn't help but think of how her story reminded me of the parable of the talents found in Matthew 25:14–30. Just like the person who was given five talents, she was a good steward of what she had been given. She stepped out and leveraged what she had; and as a result of her boldness and faith, she was able to experience God in a fresh and new way.

Another woman, Tina Hoversten, spoke next. She explained how she included her children in the challenge. Together, they decided to buy a 140 bottles of water and hand them out to public service workers doing hot jobs in their community. They made labels that included the logo for the church's campaign, "Summer 2 Serve," along with a note thanking them for serving. This simple act of kindness was well received by the sun-drenched policemen, city workers, landscapers, and construction crews. Tina and her children felt a deep joy that they were meeting a tangible need and it stirred something in them that day. Tina's eight-year-old son even asked if they could do a twenty dollar challenge every week. Tina was so changed by the challenge that she now leads a group of people who desire to serve so the cycle of service can continue in her community.

Jill Dejewski was the last person to speak. She was gut-level honest about how she missed her opportunity to leverage her twenty. She was at a garage sale where she found the lawnmower of her dreams. She and her husband Brian desperately needed a new lawnmower as theirs was on its last leg. She couldn't believe she scored and found one that was self-propelled for only twenty dollars. She quickly removed the tag off the handle, staking her claim to the lawnmower before anyone else could snag it from under her nose. She continued shopping as she envisioned herself mowing her lawn walking lazily behind this self-propelled machine of goodness. When she turned around she noticed an immigrant Latino gentleman pushing "her" lawnmower to the woman working the sale to make his purchase. Jill immediately confronted the man and explained to him that he had "her" lawnmower as she waved the tag in front of his face. Emotions started to flare as each of them made the case as to why they believed the lawnmower was theirs. Jill reluctantly gave in and let the man purchase the lawnmower. She walked away frustrated at the persistence of the Latino man and the unwillingness of the woman working the sale to intervene. It didn't hit her until she calmed down on her way home in the car.

She missed it!

The lawnmower was twenty dollars. She could have used her twenty dollars from the challenge to purchase the lawnmower for him. The realization of this saddened her. She came to class speaking authentically about the lesson God had taught her, but she was determined to give the challenge another week to see what God would do. Toward the end of the week, Jill was able to leverage her twenty dollars to help a struggling teenage girl attend a Vacation Bible School that the church was hosting the following week. The cost for the week was twenty-five dollars. In an attempt to implement the principles taught in the Sunday school class, Jill offered to help the young girl pay for twenty if she could come up with the other five. She came back later with a jar full of change equaling five dollars. Jill developed a relationship with the girl and her mother—who just happened to be the woman with cancer that Dayna had helped.

Jill's story reminded me of how God often prompts us to act when we see a need, but many times we don't listen or we miss it altogether. This happened to me when we were in Estes Park, Colorado. We were biking and we rode by a family with young children. They were all enjoying ice cream cones as they walked down the street. As I glanced at the family, I noticed that the youngest child's ice cream fell off her cone and onto the ground. She was crying as she looked down at the heap of ice cream melting on the pavement. As I watched this happen, it all seemed to take place in slow motion. It immediately crossed my mind that I should turn around, go to the ice cream shop, buy an ice cream cone, and give it to this little girl. I knew that there's a joy that comes when you're surprised by a kindness that's completely unexpected. Yet I didn't act on this prompting, and instead I rationalized that I was on a bike ride with my family and I didn't want us to be inconvenienced. While I am certain her family ended up replacing the cone, I regret that I didn't act by serving this little girl and therefore missed out on the joy of serving. It's strange, but little, seemingly insignificant regrets like this can and should have a big impact on you. They help you remember that when something bigger happens, you've got to act. How they happen for each person is a little different, but when they do happen, it's so important to act on these gut feelings. They are a prompt from God to do something for someone else.

The image of that little girl dropping her ice cream is forever etched in my memory. I made a commitment that day that whenever I felt prompted by God to act or say something, I would, even if it was an inconvenience or caused me to feel uncomfortable.

As a final challenge I stood in front of the class and held up a twenty-dollar bill from one of the participants who had given up on the challenge. I asked those in attendance to imagine that the twenty-dollar bill I was holding represented their life. I asked them to envision standing before God with Him posing the question, "How did you spend the twenty dollars I gave you?"

We all have something to give. The amount may vary from person to person, but we were given what we have not just to spend for ourselves, but so that we can bless others. When I stand before God I want to have spent my entire twenty. I don't want any change left over.

Our time in Minnesota reminded us that we are not only called to serve the poor and needy, but everyone around us. It's easy to think that poverty only includes those that are materially poor. Some of the poorest people we've met drive a BMW and live in a gated community. They may look rich on the outside, but they are poor on the inside. Many people who seemingly have it all together struggle with broken relationships or an arrogance that their money somehow sets them apart from the rest of society.

Poverty comes in many forms. While some struggle with material poverty, others struggle with relational or spiritual poverty. At the end of the day we are all called to serve and set free those held captive by poverty regardless of what form of poverty they struggle with.

Once we said good-bye to family and friends we were off to California again. While the route was familiar, so much had changed. The first time we headed west, we didn't have the foggiest idea where we were going or what would lie ahead. We still weren't sure what was around the next bend or what adventures we'd encounter on our route through the Rockies, but we knew we had found our purpose and passion.

Our mission this time wasn't just to serve those who are in need, but to inspire others to do the same. We felt equipped to empower those we inspired with tools to help them effectively serve, and we were excited to help people discover their own passion and put it into action to serve others.

32 THREE AND A HALF YEARS ON THE ROAD AND JUST GETTING STARTED

It's hard to believe that we have been on the road for three and a half years! When we embarked on this fantastic journey, none of us thought this would be the case. Oh, we may have believed we'd still be on the road, but we had no idea that all of us would still be so excited about what we are doing or that living in 340 square feet would become normal.

There are plenty of times we dream of settling down, but the funny thing is that none of us want to go back to living our old life. We don't want to go back to living in a big house or being caught up in all of our old material belongings.

We've always told the kids that if there comes a time they no longer want to be on the road, all they have to do is say the word. Every time the subject of settling down comes up, they emphatically tell us they wouldn't trade what we're doing for anything. That's the greatest confirmation we could ever imagine to confirm that we are doing exactly what we are supposed to be doing. We feel like we've crammed a lifetime of experiences into three years.

Somewhere along the road we stopped asking ourselves if we were crazy for making such a radical life change.

WHAT HAS BEEN YOUR GREATEST GROWING EXPERIENCE ON THE ROAD?

»» »» »» »» »» »» »» »» »» »» »» »» »» »» »» »» »» »» »» »»

»» BEN

When our adventure first started, it was hard for me to constantly meet new people because I was used to hanging out with the same friends, going to the same church, and never really meeting a whole lot of new people. I was always around people I was comfortable with. Being on the road has really pushed me past my comfort zone and helped me to be a more extroverted person than I was before the journey started.

»» BEKAH

The most growing experience for me is seeing how God never gives up on us. He has provided for our family in so many ways. He never lets us down, even in difficult situations when it is hard to trust Him. One time we were at a rescue mission and this lady asked if we had ever been to Disneyland. We said no, and she said that she was going to pray that we would be able to go there. I didn't really believe that we would ever get to go. But then some people that worked at Disneyland said that God literally told them to let us go for free! I was blown away at how that lady had so much faith in God.

»» ABIGAIL

The most growing experience for me would be that I feel that I am growing much closer to my family. I know that it's surprising, but most people think that we would fight more being in this small of space, but I'm actually learning to care for them more. I am also noticing that I want to serve instead of dreading the fact that we're helping others. I find myself missing serving when we need a month to get away or something.

»» NOAH

I think I've gotten friendlier, and it's easier to meet people. Just today when I was out running, I talked to five people. I feel like I'm more mature. I didn't think about homeless people when I was six, now I care about them and think about them.

We've watched our children grow so much over these past few years. Before we embarked on this incredible journey, we were inadvertently raising the kids with a slanted perception that life is about having things. We weren't necessarily keeping up with the Joneses, but our children were growing up in a typical upper-middle-class suburban bubble. Sure, we wanted to protect them from harm, but we may have been sheltering them to a fault. This lack of exposure was keeping them from experiencing all sides of life. The reality is there are real world issues and struggles people have that the kids continue to be fully exposed to since we hit the road. This realization has had a significant effect on all of our children.

We've proudly watched as each child has enhanced his or her level of confidence and sense of self in ways we didn't expect when we began this journey. It is tempting to take all the credit and chalk those changes up to great parenting; but the truth is, the changes have come from our new lifestyle and the opportunities we've provided to them to be completely comfortable in any situation with all kinds of different people.

The kids are especially grateful for the experiences we've shared because they are living life in a way most people can only dream about. After being in Africa and seeing how the children there live joyful with nothing, it was an easy decision to leave their excess behind. And in the process, each of our children has become considerably more content, less demanding, and more creative! They have learned to entertain themselves with very few toys and games and are truly thankful for whatever they get—even secondhand clothes from Goodwill.

They understand that we can't do the same things their friends' families do, such as eat out or go shopping like we used to, because we don't have a lot of extra money; but they never complain. They appreciate a family bike ride or a quiet day together spent in a park and a home-cooked meal as much as they do a fun-filled day at Sea World.

Interestingly, they also see the importance of living simply and how much time and money can be wasted without a thought. Our children will grow up understanding they don't need things to make themselves happy.

Yes, we *love* what we do and the kids will readily say they *do not* want to own a traditional home if it means having to give up the RV. At times we sure do miss the little things, like a yard to play in, a dishwasher, and separate bedrooms. Learning to adapt to our new lifestyle has taken some time and lots of flexibility, sacrifice, and discipline. We realize that living without these simple pleasures has made us more thankful and able to enjoy them all the more.

We now understand that true happiness comes from within, not from the things we own. This valuable life lesson is one of the most important gifts we as parents could help instill in our children at a young age. It wasn't planned, but it certainly became an appreciated by-product when we cut back and began living a more simple life.

We do have a dream, however, to build a ministry center where we can house the RV and have a small space for a front room, kitchen, bathroom, and a few bedrooms. It would be a place where we could rest and spread out just long enough to get rejuvenated to hit the road again, filled up to serve.

Our desire is that we would share this place with others when we are traveling, and it would also be a training center where we could equip people to make a difference in their communities through serving with dignity. We've had people throughout the country offer to help us build this facility, now we just need the land and money for the materials. Our desire is for this place to be located somewhere in or close to the Colorado mountains. We are confident that if this is in God's plan, this dream will someday be a reality.

33 EVERYONE HAS SOMETHING TO GIVE

BETH» It is my belief that we meet many teachers throughout our lifetime. There are those who teach us with their words and those who teach us by their actions; and oftentimes there are those who do both. I have had the privilege of being taught by a variety of remarkable people while we've been on the road. I've met some people who are down in life and struggling just to live each day, yet they have an inexplicable joy. Others are wealthy by the world's standard and have so much going for them, yet they are miserable. I have met those who are absolutely joyful and content with their lives, and those who never seem to find satisfaction and can never have enough. I have met homemakers to career women, people who are indulgent and self-centered, and those who are selfless and always meeting others' needs.

I used to enjoy meeting people who were just like me...who home-schooled their children, lived in the same area, and shared the same interests. I was interested and concerned about relating to others. Now, I seek out the opposite—people who are not like me—because I now cherish the value of learning from others, from their successes, mistakes, and experiences.

My life has been truly enriched by hearing other people's challenges and life stories. When we lived in a traditional home, we were surrounded by many of the same types of people every day. We all lived in a similar neighborhood, drove expensive cars, and had similar lives. On one hand, there is a simple comfort that comes from that; on the other hand, Jay and I are wired in such a way that we actually get a thrill out of the experience of meeting new people—especially those who are different from us. I think that's one of the many reasons that life on the road fits us. Meeting new people can make a potentially mundane day into an exciting and sometimes entertaining one, just from engaging in a conversation with someone who is unique or intriguing.

We've enjoyed meeting all types of people—conservative, free-spirited, radical, traditional, educated, homeless—because each have their own unique perspective and view of life, one I am always interested in hearing. To us, that process of getting to know someone is far more enjoyable than talking about myself, which I continue to struggle with, even while writing this book.

We can learn so much from others if we are simply willing to take the time to ask questions and to truly listen to what people have to say.

One woman I'll never forget is a single mom who was struggling to make ends meet. Her husband was unfaithful and left her for another woman. It was obvious that she was heartbroken as she shared her tearful story openly and easily with me. Her life had been dramatically altered by this sudden change of events. She was clearly struggling to figure out how to live this new and unexpected life—a life she would have never chosen and was not prepared for but that she now found herself knee deep in.

As she comfortingly hugged the sweater that was draped around her shoulders, she explained to me that she was not bitter or resentful. She had a justifiable, ethical, righteous anger; but she was not bitter. She was beautiful; and as tears rolled out of her bright blue eyes, I couldn't help but fix my thoughts on her children and the effect this was most likely having on them. Her teenage daughter, who was standing nearby, captivated me by her porcelain doll-like features. I witnessed her despondently lower her head in shame while her mother told me everything she'd endured. Her rejection seemed to be what stung the most.

Her experience taught me to treasure all that I have. Sometimes I can be critical of Jay and grumble about things that don't matter in the scope of life. I can get ruthlessly focused on his imperfections, reminding him of them more often than I'd like to admit. It's unfair to expect unconditional love, forgiveness, and grace from him yet hold him to a standard of perfection—something none of us can ever live up to all the time. I have met a scattering of people whose lives have been touched by divorce, infidelity, separation, abuse, and the alienation that accompanies these. When I listen to these stories, it is as if someone is placing a megaphone to my ear and is shouting at me to truly love, cherish, appreciate, nurture, enjoy, and be thankful for what I have.

I have been blessed with a loving and devoted husband. He is a good man, and he is faithful and cares deeply about our marriage and our kids. I am blessed beyond belief. I am learning how to hold dear to what I have, to treasure our marriage and not take it for granted. I am learning to overlook the little things and to enjoy each and every day, for none of us knows what tomorrow holds.

Another woman I had the pleasure of spending time with in California, Gina, has a passion to share the timeless tradition of English tea with those she loves. It unexpectedly began when she asked a friend of hers how she would like to celebrate her birthday. Her friend insisted on having a tea party. Gina initially objected but then realized this was her friend's birthday and she wanted it to be a blessing to her. Little did she know that this was going to be the beginning of a beautiful new passion she would later pass on to many others.

As Gina and I walked through her home and she allowed me to page through her tea photo album and her books about tea and faith, I was surprised to find myself genuinely caught up in her world. Little did I know, this was not just a passion or a hobby, it was a bridge she used to reach out and touch those in her life who were elderly, widowed, or in need of friendship or a listening ear. She had grasped the art of slowing down, enjoying simple conversation, and loving the elegant things in life. As we walked through her dining room, she showed me her beautiful collection of unique and interesting tea dishes neatly held in a beautiful china cabinet.

Because Gina desired that the elderly women she met with would not have to fuss with dirty dishes or crumbs, she found a way to pack all of her necessary items into a rolling cart—and she brings the tea party to them. She brings everything needed for a charming tea, including a beautiful tablecloth, delicate dishes, napkins, flowers, candles, elaborate treats, hot tea in a thermos, beautiful tea pot, and even English hats! Her enthusiasm was contagious, and I suddenly realized this was something I could implement in my own life. The art of slowing down, sipping hot tea, and listening to another woman of any age share her life with me. Isn't this something we could all use in our busy lives?

Many times when I meet a friend, we find a nearby coffee shop or a simple restaurant. We talk and catch up on life events together. However, when Gina treated my girls and me to a real traditional tea, I grasped the vast difference between the two. The scenery was beautiful and peaceful. We were out on her patio; the hummingbirds and flowers were around us. There were no crowds and no loud coffee machines in the background. It was perfect for sharing intimacy.

I truly found myself coming alive with ideas on how I could use this to be a ministry to others. Gina explained that it doesn't have to be elaborate. Just the simple touch of flowers or even store-bought scones on pretty dishes does the trick.

Since our afternoon tea with Gina, I have enjoyed teatime with my daughters as a beautiful way for us to connect and slow down in our fast-paced life. I continue to look for opportunities to use the treasured gift of tea as a way to celebrate and nurture friendships and as a ministry to those who are hurting or lonely. In our short three months together, Gina shared several of her gifts and talents with me; and each time, I left encouraged about the many ways we can use our passions to benefit others.

Another woman I met who touched my life was struggling with her teenage daughter—up to this point, something I haven't had to deal with. In tears, she opened up to me that her heart ached to have a relationship with her daughter; but she felt helpless, as her daughter was walking down the wrong path and making poor choices in her life by hanging out with the wrong crowd and rebelling against her parents. I sat with her and listened as I thought back on my days as a teenager too. She was sharing deep hurts and regrets, and although I have not walked in her shoes as a mother, I knew I could offer her a compassionate ear because I was surely very much like her daughter at the same age.

When I left our conversation, I retraced many of the things she shared, the opportunities she felt like she had missed along the way, the questions and regrets she had, and so much more. I thought of my own life with two teenagers and two more in the making.

What could I be doing right now to build my relationship with them to make it stronger than it is now?

I know I won't do it all perfectly, and that I can't ensure that they won't make wrong choices or rebel; but I was positive I had something to learn from her openness and her experience so I too would be able to draw on this if the day comes when I have to deal with my children as they experience their own growing pains.

The people who have had the most profound effect on me were the ones who shared their life honestly and openly and also took the time to ask questions and listen when we responded. I love sitting in someone's home, hearing her stories. I love to see how others live life. That is fascinating to me, to watch how couples interact with each other, how they parent their children, how they live their day-to-day life with their set of responsibilities, how they juggle their personal life with work and other commitments. We can learn so much if we just take a step back and observe, listen, absorb, and allow ourselves to be taught by others.

WHAT DO YOU ENJOY MOST ABOUT BEING ON THE ROAD?

»» »»

»» BEN Wow! I enjoy a lot of things! One is being able to see all different parts of the country. From New York City to Newport Beach, California, its been a really amazing experience. Another is meeting lots of different people and friends across the country!

»» BEKAH The thing I most enjoy about being on the road is getting to serve those in need. I feel like we are helping them instead of turning our heads and pretending we didn't see them.

»» ABIGAIL The thing that I enjoy most about being on the road would definitely have to be sightseeing. Another thing that I enjoy is serving. There are some extraordinary people under some of those bridges. It is so good to see people come out from under the bridges. To just think that they are starting a new life brings joy to my heart.

»» NOAH Being with my family, meeting people, and going to cool museums and seeing things.

CHALLENGE #10
Everyone Has Something to Give

»» »» »» »» »» »» »» »» »» »» »» »» »» »» »» »» »» »» »»

Regardless of our status in life or how much we have, we all have something to give. We often think of giving as only financial. When you boil it down, the most important thing in life is relationships—our relationships with God, our families, and those who surround us. All of us can offer a listening ear, a warm hug, or a word of encouragement. Some of the most relationally rich people we know make their home under a bridge. They have learned the secret of living in community and sharing all that they have.

It's easy to get overwhelmed when we look out and see all the problems that surround us. Homelessness, poverty, sickness, and disease—the problems just seem too big, so we become paralyzed and do nothing. We need to remember the words of Mother Teresa, who said, "We can do no great things, only small things with great love." Imagine how different the world would be if we each began to act on what we know and gave what we could, however small it might seem.

Just imagine if the boy mentioned in John 6 wouldn't have been willing to give his lunch to Jesus. He could have easily assumed that the five loaves and two fish that he had in his lunch were simply too small to offer to Jesus. He could have thought, "This crowd is simply too enormous and too hungry for my lunch to make a difference." Because he gave the little that he had, Jesus was able to multiply it and feed more than five thousand people.

» What do you have to give to others?
» Will you give what you have, no matter how small it may seem?

We challenge you to give your five loaves and two fish and see how God can multiply what you give.

34 OUR CALL TO ACTION

We realize that many of you reading this book feel a nagging tug in your life that you were meant for more. We know that our story may be unique, but our desires are not. We believe each and every one of us wants our lives to matter. We all want to find significance and purpose. Don't ignore that feeling deep inside you. Listen to the still, small voice of God and quiet yourself long enough to discover how He has made you and discover how He wants to use your life.

As we reflect on our journey, we realize that this dream didn't develop overnight. It took time. God planted a seed, a thought, in the early years of our relationship to travel and to one day share our story. He then spent the first ten years of our marriage overhauling our lives, healing the past, and changing our beliefs. The ten years following that were spent rebuilding our health, our marriage, and the unity in our family life. We now see the necessary process that God had to take us through to get us to the point where we were ready to jump off the cliff and into the unknown. Had it happened to us any sooner, it could have been disastrous to our family. We now see how God's timing is truly perfect.

When we began our journey, our desire was simple: simplify our lives and serve those in need. In the beginning, we romanticized what serving would be like. We imagined parking in homeless areas, building relationships, giving free haircuts, popping popcorn, and having a movie playing on a projector hanging from the RV. Never did we imagine the hardships—having nowhere to park, struggling financially, and battling the unfamiliar surroundings and the uncertainty of our future. We never expected the mortgage business to dissipate or our simple desire to show acts of random kindness to turn into a ministry mobilizing others to serve. We didn't realize that the unceasing feeling that God had something more for us meant starting a nonprofit and becoming organizers and teachers. We just simply went out with the sole purpose of obeying what God was laying on our hearts.

Finding our passion and purpose was exhilarating and liberating. We liken it to taking a horse who for years had only been allowed to roam around in a limited, fenced-in yard and one day, unexpectedly unlatching the gate and letting him run out into the countryside, unhindered and unrestricted. The freedom and fulfillment we have experienced have been worth more than any valuable thing we could have possessed on earth. The satisfaction is an intangible, indescribable richness that we wouldn't exchange.

We marvel now as we look at how God has held our hand, guided us, and helped us to build a strong marriage, family, and ministry. To see the beautiful children He has entrusted us with, to instill principles in them and watch as they grow and find their own passion, and to see how our marriage continues to blossom. We are in awe of the many deep relationships we formed across the country that continue to bring us encouragement. We are grateful for those who have walked beside us, championed our cause, believed in our family, and invested in our ministry. We have just begun to catch a glimpse of what He wants for our lives. Because we have seen how big God is and how He continues to amaze us and do much more than we ever thought or imagined, we know that there is more ahead on this journey and we hold tightly to Him in hopeful anticipation as we join Him in His work.

Although it took us years to get to where we are today, it may not be the same for you. We believe that God has uniquely gifted each person with skills, abilities, and passions; and He wants to use them to bless and help others. Each person's journey will look different, just as each of our gifts and abilities are unique and different. We encourage you to see how God empowers you to serve others with dignity and discover what your passion is and how uniquely gifted you are.

God cares about you deeply, and He wants to direct and guide you. He doesn't want you to spend a lifetime wandering around in the dark wondering what your purpose is. His guidance, wisdom, and direction are at your fingertips; and He wants to be intimately involved in your life. He spends our entire lifetime pursuing us and changing us from the inside out. He never gives up; and throughout our lives, we see evidence that He has been moving us steadily in the direction He wants us to go. Remember that He is always at work. All of life is a journey, and He promises to build us and work in us and through us until the day when we come face to face with Him.

If you feel dissatisfied with your life, don't shove the feeling down, slap on a smile, and ignore it. It may be God making you uncomfortable because He has another purpose for your life. He may be causing the discontentment or discouragement with your current situation as a catalyst to move you into something far greater.

Don't feel discouraged if the changes you want to see in your life aren't coming. They will. Be patient and trust that God knows best and that He will lead you into what He has for you in His timing. Continue to serve and do something right where you are. Don't wait for that "someday." You can do something today.

You can volunteer at your local homeless shelter, visit shut-ins, go to the local nursing home, or deliver a meal to a sick neighbor. The opportunities to serve are endless, and they are right outside your door. What's more, the principles in this book—about discovering your unique dream, doing extraordinary things, giving selflessly—are applicable in the broad realm of everyday life, not just in charitable service or community volunteering.

In the meantime, consider your specific gifts. Are you good at art, teaching, basketball, photography, networking, or business skills? What do you like to do in your free time? What excites you and makes your heart race? What bothers you or makes you angry: prostitution, AIDS, abandoned children, starvation? We encourage you to take time to recognize your uniqueness and your passions and how God has uniquely made you; and in that, you will discover His purpose for you. We also invite you to work through the study we've written which is designed to empower you to serve others with dignity and help you discover what your passion is and how you can leverage it to serve others.

We believe that what has begun is more than a ministry or an organization—it's a movement that is happening everywhere. It's an emerging part of the world of believers everywhere. A movement of ordinary, average people who are tired of the status quo and life as normal.

We're just a family of six, but if we can inspire others to break out of their comfort zones, pursue their dreams, push past fear, and act on what they know—how the world could be different.

The foundation of Passion to Action is the passion that God has for us and the passion we have for Him. When we understand how crazy and relentless He is for us and we get filled up with His love and pursue a deep personal relationship with Him, then and only then will our service have power. His love is what fills and sustains us.

Will you discover your dream and passion?

Are you willing to risk something and break past your fear?

If so, then we invite you to join us by putting *your* passion to action!

10 CHALLENGES

P2A Challenge #1 — God Gives Each of Us a Unique Dream and Passion

We believe that before the creation of time the God of the universe plants a unique dream and passion in each of us to be used for His glory. He has given us a unique set of skills and abilities.

The questions you must answer are: What is your dream? What do you have a passion for? What skills and abilities do you have that you can use to help others?

We challenge you to pursue your dream, identify your passion, and use your God-given talents to serve others.

»»

P2A Challenge #2 — God Works All around Us

Let's face it, God is big. He doesn't need your help accomplishing anything. The same God who created the universe, closed the mouths of lions, and opened the Red Sea is working all around you today. He's quite capable on His own; however, He invites you to join Him in the work that He's doing. Will you quiet yourself, be still, and ask Him to guide you?

Will you listen to His response and act on what He shows you?

We challenge you to accept His incredible invitation to partner with Him in the work He is doing all around you.

»»

P2A Challenge #3 — Faith Is the Key to Breaking through Fear

Fear and faith are roommates. When you exercise your faith and do something that involves considerable risk, you will face fear. David must have experienced fear when he stood before Goliath with five stones and a measly sling shot.

What fears do you face as you step out in faith?

Will you remind yourself as David did how God has protected and provided for you in the past?

What declaration will you make?

We challenge you to step out in faith and risk something for God.

»»

P2A Challenge #4 — God Uses Ordinary People to Do Extraordinary Things

Everything is opposite with God. He loves to use the weak and broken things in the world to astound the wise. You may think your life is a complete mess, and you wonder how anything good can come from your past. The truth is that God is able to take the broken pieces of your life and build a beautiful mosaic that displays His love and grace.

Will you allow God to take all the broken pieces of your past and allow Him to create something beautiful with your life?

We challenge you to give Him your life and see what He can create. He has the ability to take the ordinary and make it extraordinary.

»»

P2A Challenge #5 — Everyone Matters

We live in a society that is consumed with how we look. We are obsessed with our outward appearance without taking the time to nurture our inner selves. Because we focus on the external, we tend to group ourselves with others of similar backgrounds, life circumstances, as well as socio-economic statuses. It becomes easy to label people, especially those who are far different from us. Since everyone matters to God, everyone should matter to us, regardless of their appearance or the perceived role that they play in society. Everyone is worthy of dignity and respect because we are all made in the image of God.

Will you begin to view people the way God sees them and get to know them for who they really are inside?

We challenge you to go out of your way and extend your hand to someone who looks far different from you.

P2A Challenge #6 — When You Give, You Get So Much in Return

One of the biggest perks in serving is that it brings joy. It's common to think that when you serve, someone else's life will be changed; but inevitably, you are the one who is changed and who receives more in the end.

We invite you to step out and experience the joy of giving.

We challenge you to give to those who can't repay you and then be ready to receive much more than you give.

»»»

P2A Challenge #7 — Unified Families Reflect God's Perfect Relationship with Himself

Unified families reflect God's perfect relationship with Himself. When a family loves each other and serves together, they reflect God's light to the people around them. They are like a bonfire to a world in need. Just as a fire draws you to its warmth and causes you to be mesmerized by its flame, so does the unified family that serves together.

Let's face it, maintaining family unity and loving those closest to you takes a lot of work.

Will you strive for unity in your family?

Will you love your family and be a conduit to reflect God's light?

We challenge you to serve together as a family and see how God uses your lives to shine like a huge bonfire to the world around you.

»»»

P2A Challenge #8 — Life Is Short, Eternity Is Long

There are only two things that will last for eternity: God and people. With that in mind the only thing that matters in this life is how we love God and those that surround us. Nothing else will last.

Will you live your life in such a way that you will have no regrets on that day?

Will you live each day with eternity in mind?

We challenge you to love God with all your heart, mind, and strength and to love those around you as if today was the last day of your life.

P2A Challenge #9 — We All Live God's Story

Your story is all about God. It's about His glory and everything points to Him. The crazy thing is that He chooses to write you into His story. He's the central figure and the main character. You simply play a supporting role in His story.

Regardless of who you are, God wants to speak to you. You don't have to be a scholar or a saint to hear His voice. You simply need to be still. He will speak to you. He's concerned about your life, and He wants to use it to do something significant for Him.

He's inviting you into His story.

Will you accept His role and script for your life?

We challenge you to know your lines in your role by quieting yourself, being still, and listening for His voice.

»»

P2A Challenge #10 — Everyone Has Something to Give

Regardless of your status in life or how much you have, we all have something to give. We often think of giving as only financial. When you boil it down, the most important thing in life is relationships: our relationships with God, our families, and those who surround us. All of us can offer a listening ear, a warm hug, or a word of encouragement. It's easy to get overwhelmed when we look out and see all the problems that surround us. Homelessness, poverty, sickness, and disease—the problems just seem too big, so we become paralyzed and do nothing.

What do you have to give to others?

Will you give what you have, no matter how small it may seem?

We challenge you to give your five loaves and two fish and see how God can multiply what you give.

ACKNOWLEDGMENTS

There have been so many people we've met on our journey who have loved and supported our family and our mission. The number of relationships and friendships that we've developed over the past three and a half years is staggering. We are indebted to so many people who have shown us amazing kindness and love. Even as we attempt to acknowledge those who have invested in us, we are sure it's inevitable we will fail to mention someone. With that in mind, we apologize in advance for anyone we leave out.

Laura Morton, a good friend and trusted advisor, without whom this book would not be possible. Thank you for all of the long hours you spent putting our "moving target" story to print. The entire team at Guideposts Books; David Morris, Carl Raymond, Jason Rovenstine, Joanie Garborg, Carlton Garborg, Randy Elliott and Debbie Felt, for your input, direction, and for believing in our mission. We are grateful for your support and wisdom! Mel Berger, a real pro to whom we are grateful, and as well for your team at William Morris Endeavor.

David and Denise, for your friendship and for investing so generously in our mission. Randy Walton, David Saylor, and Jim Horn, for serving on the P2A Board. We value your counsel and wisdom. Brad Lenardson (Rebel), Brad Wolfe (The Wolf) and Wynn Smiley, for walking alongside of us and providing support and friendship by serving on our Team of Advocates. If we ever end up in a foxhole, we want you beside us!

Matt and Ang Toth, for your incredible love for Jesus that constantly inspires us to press deeper into the heart of God. We love what you and Toth Ministries (www.tothministries.org) stand for.

Mark Morse and the entire team at MorseKode (www.morsekode. com), for your talent and creativity. We are so indebted to you for all your help with our branding and website. Joe Beard, for always being there for us when we have a question about video. Not only are you a creative beast but a great friend. Dru Dalton and Real Thread (www.realthread. com), for amazing T-shirts that are also good for the environment— what?! Kristi Piehl at Media Minefield (www.media-minefield.com), for your amazing talent with our P2A video and your incredible heart. Lee Zweifelhofer, for your wicked videography editing skills. Thanks for all the hours you put in creating the P2A video and connecting us to your neighbor Tim Buzza, who created a killer custom music bed.

Dr. Beaber and your office at Beaber Family Orthodontics, for your generosity and the amazing smiles of Bekah, Abigail, and Noah.

Richard Vernon, for helping kick-start our service. George and Casey Wood, your generosity and love for our family. Your story of perseverance and love for each other is astonishing.

Phil Hissom, for investing time in teaching us community development principles. Our ministry is better off because of your input. Isma Martinez, for being such a wonderful example of someone who uses their giftedness to serve others. Thanks for helping us anytime we need design help all the way from Spain. Mike Huffstatler, for your outstanding skills in the photography department.

Jason and Natalie Snapp, for your time, talent, and treasure. You leveraged all three of them to bless our family. Jason, you are the dentist extraordinaire; and, Natalie, your feedback from reading through the manuscript was incredibly valuable and insightful.

Brian and Jen Wiegers, for your authenticity and love. Thanks for being such strong advocates of our family and ministry. Eddie Moratin, for being the most connected person we know in Orlando. We are grateful for your strategic insight to us during some extremely formative times of Passion to Action.

Brian Johansson, your input, honesty, and wisdom were so timely—and not by accident!—with all that we were walking through when we met. Don and Cyndie Truax, for your encouraging company in Charlotte. Because of your action Beth was able to see her dad one last time. Jared Yaple, for being so supportive of what we do and for your feedback on the manuscript. We love what's happening with Start (www.juststart.org).

To everyone who's allowed us to stay in your home or park the RV at your home or location: Jim and Corey Corbet, Dave and Linda Johnson, John and Jill Turner, Cummins, Newport Dunes RV Resort, Mountain Lakes RV Resort, Jerry and Rachelle Brand, Randy and April Stensgard, Jim and Lynn Matthews, Mariners Church, New Vintage Church, Troy and Jennifer Schrock, Gerald and Liesa Martinez, Jen and Dennis Hoglin, Dwight and Gina Hanson, Life Assembly, Mike and Janice Reeves, the Bowery Mission, Steve and Bridget Hunt, Gwen Whitten, Claudio and Gina Medina, Heartland Presbyterian Center, New Life Church, Waterstone Church, Bryan Loecken, Jerry and JoAnn Loecken, Niagara Bible Conference, Randy and Crista Walton, Bud and Val Worthing, Matthews United Methodist Church, Camper Village, Maple Hill Estates, Marg and Jim Rehnberg, Art and Marti Horwitz, Tom and Cindy Toth, Paul and Wendy Standinger.

Last but not least we are incredibly grateful for the team of financial supporters who invest in the vision of Passion to Action. Your generous gifts allow us to continue inspiring, empowering, and mobilizing people to live in action.

》》

Visit **Passiontoaction.org** to discover more about the authors and their ministry. You'll find videos, blogs, photos, Facebook and Twitter links, and a way to contact the authors and invite them to speak at your church, event, or group. You'll also find an online Passion to Action store and information about additional resources, including a small group study guide.

》》